Making
Winning Presentations

Making
Winning
Presentations

*How to carry the day with
confidence and success*

GHASSAN HASBANI
2nd edition

How To Books

Published by How To Books Ltd, 3 Newtec Place,
Magdalen Road, Oxford OX4 1RE. United Kingdom.
Tel: (01865) 793806. Fax: (01865) 248780.
email: info@howtobooks.co.uk
http://www.howtobooks.co.uk

First edition 1996
Second edition 1999

British Library Cataloguing in Publication Data
A catalogue record for this book is available from
the British Library

Cover design by Shireen Nathoo Design
Cover image PhotoDisc
Cartoons by Mike Flanagan

Produced for How To Books by Deer Park Productions
Typeset by PDQ Typesetting, Stoke-on-Trent, Staffs.
Printed and bound by Cromwell Press, Trowbridge, Wiltshire

NOTE: The material contained in this book is set out in good
faith for general guidance and no liability can be accepted
for loss or expense incurred as a result of relying in particular
circumstances on statements made in the book. The laws and
regulations are complex and liable to change, and readers should
check the current position with the relevant authorities before
making personal arrangements.

Contents

List of Illustrations

Preface
to the Second Edition

'Good communication skills' is a phrase repeatedly used in job descriptions and CVs. These skills can make or break people's careers and are highly regarded by employers and organisations.

One of the most important communication skills is the ability to present and put your ideas across whether you are an employee or an independent consultant, a civil servant or business person, a school teacher or a university lecturer, a member of the local club or someone starting a career in politics. No matter who you are or what kind of work you do, you always need to communicate with people on different occasions and present to them ideas, news or achievements.

Lack of confidence is one of the most common problems found among individuals, or groups, when faced with the task of giving a presentation. To combat the fear of this monster called 'Presenting', you need to get to know more about it, which will make you realise that it isn't a monster after all.

Being able to generate ideas is a very important asset in developing your career, but the ability to present these ideas to other people and make them understand them or agree with them gives you a competitive edge. It is hoped this book will help you achieve this competitive edge yourself.

Ghassan Hasbani

1

Getting Your Message Across

Presentations are very powerful communication tools. They can be used in a multitude of situations to get a message across effectively. They vary in size and importance, depending on the occasion and the subject of the presentation.

Throughout your career, you may find yourself presenting under different circumstances, to different types of people. This chapter will give you a few examples of situations where you may find yourself addressing a group of people or even one person, to put a message across and make them agree with or believe what you tell them.

There is a general process that you can follow, to produce a winning presentation. You can adapt this process to suit any situation you find yourself presenting in. This process is shown in Figure 1.

SELLING A NEW PRODUCT

One of the most common presentation skill applications is selling. Whether it is a new product, service or concept, the same techniques apply.

Selling a product can sometimes be very simple. This is when the buyer does not need any convincing and wants to buy the product, simply because he or she is attracted to it or wants it desperately.

In many cases, you need to convince your customers that your product or idea is what they really want. A presentation offers you the opportunity to talk to your customers, introduce the product to them and tell them how it can help meet their needs or requirements.

What goes into a sales presentation

A good way to present a new product is to tell your customers what it is and what it can do to help them solve their problems or fulfil their requirements. The structure of your presentation should meet

13

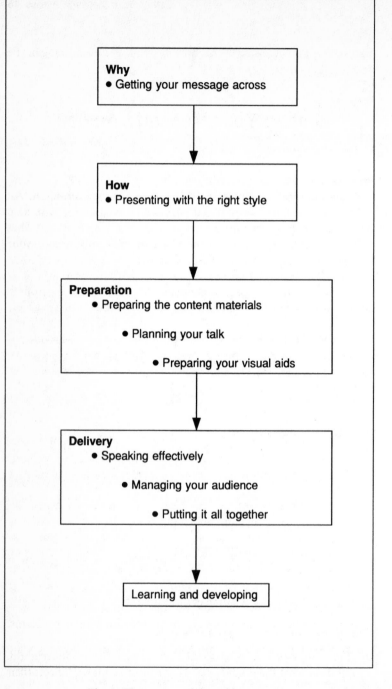

Fig. 1. The presentation making process.

these criteria. An example of how a sales presentation can be structured is outlined opposite:

Subject
- Start by stating what the subject of your presentation is.

- Introduce yourself at this point.

Presentation objectives
- Tell them what you want to achieve from your presentation. An example could be: 'I would like to introduce you to the new version of...' or 'I hope, by this presentation, to give you an idea of what our product can do and how you can use it to reduce your operational costs.'

- If your objective contains several points, or you have more than one objective, use bullet points and create a short list on your slide or flip chart.

Audience needs or requirements
Tell them what you think their needs are.

- Be general and don't go into too many details. You do this to make them think about their needs.

- Ask them what they think their needs are. After you have made them give some thought to their requirements, it is time for them to tell you what they want, or think they want. Remember, you want to sell them what they want as opposed to what you think they want.

How the product meets these needs
- Use a series of slides or flip chart pages for this section if required.

- Tell them about the features of your product that meet these needs and how this product can help them solve their problems.

- Don't drift into a detailed explanation of what the product can do. Tell them what the product can do for them and how it meets their needs.

Main benefits
- Go through the benefits the product can offer your customers.

- Discuss the financial benefits to the customers. Finance is always a key issue when looking into a new product, so make sure you don't ignore it.

- If there is another product in direct competition with yours, and the customers seem to be keen on discussing the subject, highlight the cost benefits between your product and the competitor's.

Summary
Summarise what you have told them, highlighting the main issues that are relevant to the particular customer.

Actions required
- Tell your audience what the next step is going to be.

- Answer any questions they might have.

Leave mentioning the price till the end and preferably until asked about it. Remind your customers of the benefits they will get from the product or service before giving them the price.

Doing it yourself
Choose a service, product or idea. Now, think of a customer that you know about very well. Go through each of the above headings and prepare a short presentation to sell your service, idea or product to that customer. When you have finished, indicate, in the table below, the level of difficulty you encountered in creating each section.

This exercise will help you identify the sections that you need to spend more time on when preparing a presentation in a real life situation. Sections which score 3 or more are the ones that need more attention.

Section	*Level of difficulty*				
Objectives	1	2	3	4	5
Customer needs	1	2	3	4	5
Meeting their needs	1	2	3	4	5
Benefits	1	2	3	4	5
Summary	1	2	3	4	5

How can I ask the customers to tell me what they want if, in some cases, they don't know themselves?
If your customers are not sure of what they want, help them find out. Make them more familiar with your product or service, then suggest a few main areas where they can look for improvement in their operations.

PRESENTING AT A JOB INTERVIEW

How many job interviews have you had in your life so far? Have you ever thought of them as presentations? Well, there's always a first time.

A job interview can be treated as a presentation with the main subject being you. You are trying to sell yourself to the potential employer. You need to present to them your skills and personal qualities to show them that you can fit within their team or fulfil the job requirements.

When you receive the invitation for an interview, you need to do the following:

1. Get more information about the employer and write a short report about them for your own personal use.

2. Prepare an agenda for the interview. Although you may not have total control over the conversation, you can always have a few topics ready in your mind to mention.

3. Put together a file about yourself. This may include a summary of activities you participated in, previous work that you are proud of, certificates and awards, etc. Show this to the interviewer, as it helps him or her form a more informed opinion of you.

Giving a presentation at the interview

You may decide to actually give a presentation during the interview. If the facilities are available and can be arranged beforehand, why not? In fact, some employers now request a short presentation from their job applicants. This can leave a very good impression on the interviewer if done properly. In order to do it well, you need to remember the following:

• Start by introducing yourself and giving your personal details.

- Give a short introduction on what aspect of your previous experience you want to talk about.

- Go through the events and experiences one by one, showing what you learned from them. Avoid reading out a list of courses and jobs that you have done. What you learned from a certain position is more important than the job title.

- Emphasise the experience or qualifications that are relevant to the job you are applying for.

- Give the employer your suggestions on how you can positively contribute to their operations. For this, you need to use the information you found out earlier about the organisation.

- For each idea you suggest, make sure you have a very valid argument for back-up.

Make a list of the five most important skills and achievements you can mention at a job interview. How would you present them at the interview?

How can I give a presentation in a job interview if I do not have the facilities?
If you don't have the facilities to use visual aids, take with you relevant documents that are evidence of your previous achievements, and show them to the interviewer. These act as your visual aids, as you take the person, or group of people, through the details.

PRESENTING UNPOPULAR INFORMATION

How many times have you attended a presentation to hear that some cuts are going to take place in your department or some people are going to be made redundant? Have you ever had to be the bearer of bad news?

The presentation layout
In a situation like this, you need to structure your presentation in a way that reduces the negative impact of the news on the audience and reassures them about what is going to happen in the future.

This may be done as follows:

Introduction
This includes the subject of your discussion and your name, if your face is not familiar to most of your audience.

The current situation
- State the bad news in the least shocking manner. Tell them straight away what is happening and don't try to waffle your way through.

- Be direct and use vocabulary that is easy to understand.

Reasons for the bad news
- Take them through the sequence of events that led to this situation.

- Tell them the reasons for taking that decision.

- Discuss the alternatives to the decision that has been made, stating the pros and cons of each course of action.

What next
- Talk about the series of actions and events that will take place in the future to implement the decision.

- Discuss how these actions will address the problem.

- Tell them how your plan is going to make life less complicated and facilitate the change process.

The future
- Remind everybody of the vision set out for the future by the group or organisation.

- Set a clear goal for the future and attach a time-scale to it.

- Remind your audience that this is a fresh start and that they now need to look forward to future achievements.

Summary
Use the summary to remind them of the key points, especially the

positive ones which will make them more enthusiastic and looking forward to future success. Morale is usually down after hearing any kind of bad news, so try to boost their morale with a positive summary and conclusion.

> Can you think of three different types of bad news that can be communicated to a group of people? Consider examples from your past experience or imagination.

LECTURING

The word 'lecturing' can have negative associations. 'Don't lecture me' is often used by some people when they are being told off, or given long and patronising advice. This is probably due to the traditional boring nature of lectures, which take the form of a long talk by one person, rarely interrupted by a question or two which don't really get answered.

Giving a successful lecture

To give a successful lecture, you need to always remember that you are trying to teach the audience something. You want them to leave the room knowing more about the subject than when they came in. This is easier said than done.

A lecture is a presentation, preferably an interactive one. Try to structure it and include the points that you want to get across and nothing else. It is very easy to drift into additional explanations, because you know quite a lot about the subject, and forget the aim of your lecture. A good lecture can be structured as follows:

Introduction
- If you are not known by the audience, introduce yourself and tell them about your background. This gives them more confidence in you, unless you don't have the right background.

- State the title and the subject of your lecture.

- Tell your audience what to expect to learn from the session.

- Ask them if there are any specific areas they would like you to concentrate on.

Contents
- Introduce the topics to be covered and the proportion of the total time allocated to each of them.

- Provide an overall description of the subject and explain how the topics of discussion fit together.

Language
Define any major terms that you feel are important for them to understand, before you start. At this stage, it is not recommended that you go through a long list of terms and definitions, because it is not likely that your audience will remember them all.

Topics of discussion
Start by discussing the topics one by one. For each of the topics:

- Go through the details and put your points across.

- Give examples and case studies, if applicable, or any historical events associated with it.

- If you know a funny story or remark which is relevant to the subject, mention it. This helps the audience remember your point by associating it with the story.

- Try to make your lecture interactive. Ask questions and write down the answers where everyone can see them. If you don't get the right answers, you can always tell them your own version.

- Give your audience little exercises to work on. This helps them remember what you taught them and stay awake for the next topic. These exercises will also act as short breaks if the lecture is too long.

Summary and conclusion
- Remind the audience of the purpose of the lecture and what has been learned.

- Relate the subject of your lecture to real life situations and how the theory can be applied in practice.

- Answer any final questions which may have resulted from the lecture and could not be asked under any specific topic.

- Tell the audience about sources of information and further reading related to the subject.

- Thank everyone for their attention and tell them about the next session, if applicable.

How can I give my students practical exercises and still have enough time to go though the lecture material in one session?
Reduce the amount of information you are trying to put across in the lecture. Use notes and handouts for detailed information and highlight the important points of your talk. They can then refer to the notes when doing the exercises and learn more this way.

CHECKLIST

1. The aim of a sales presentation is to persuade your customers that your product will meet their needs.

2. A job interview can be thought of as a presentation where the aim is to sell yourself.

3. In presenting 'bad news', it is vital to reduce the negative impact, and emphasise the positive, forward-looking points.

4. The main purpose of a lecture is to teach the audience something.

CASE STUDIES

Brian sells his services

Brian is a computer expert. He specialises in developing databases for organisations of different sizes. He sets up a meeting with a company that specialises in selling computer products, to try to sell them his services. He gives them a presentation and starts by introducing himself and telling them about his expertise. Then he highlights the fact that they need to hold more information about their customers, so they can cater better for their demands and needs. He then asks the group to come up with a list of problems they think need solving. After a few minutes, they tell him what they think they need.

He takes the list and goes through it item by item, highlighting the ways he can help solve their problem by providing them with a database tailored to suit their needs. Towards the end, they ask him for the cost and he gives them a rough estimate based on the information he obtained from the meeting. He manages to sell his services.

John lectures his students, but doesn't teach them

John is a new lecturer at a college of further education. He is responsible for teaching a group of twenty students. On his first day, he enters the classroom and starts immediately with the first lecture.

The students start looking at their timetable to find out what the subject is supposed to be, from the scheduled lessons. Half an hour later and after a very boring talk, all they can hear is echoes and mumbling, a clear indication that they are starting to fall asleep. They leave the room without learning anything.

Miriam gets a job

Miriam is a recent graduate looking for an interesting job. To tell the truth, any job. She receives an invitation to be interviewed by a company that she really wants to work for.

She phones the human resources department and asks them if they can provide an overhead projector in the interviewing room, so she can give the interviewer a short presentation. They like the idea very much, and promise to provide her with what she has asked for.

She arrives on time and introduces herself. She gives the panel of interviewers a short presentation about the ways she can contribute to their operations using the skills she has. Being a recent graduate, she doesn't have many skills, so Miriam also mentions how she is ready to learn new skills to develop into a more effective role. She also presents evidence of her ability to learn quickly. They ask her a few questions and answer her queries. Two days later, Miriam receives a phone call from human resources, offering her the job.

POINTS TO CONSIDER

1. What is the purpose of a presentation and what are the different steps in the general process of preparing and giving a presentation?

2. How could John have improved his performance in the lecture?

3. What do you need to understand or know about your customers, before offering them your solution?

4. When breaking bad news, what do you need to do before the end of your presentation?

5. What do you think helped Miriam secure the job she wanted, even though she wasn't highly skilled?

6. How can you reinforce what you teach in a lecture and, at the same time, keep the audience interested?

7. How can you use your presentation skills to secure a new job?

8. What do you need to include in your presentation to a potential employer?

2

Presenting the Right Style

COMMUNICATING WITH PEOPLE

One of the most useful natural skills we have, is the ability to communicate using different languages. This amazing ability is not limited to speech only, but extends to visual elements too, such as **body language**. Our body language can say a great deal. Facial expressions, hand movements and posture are all related to how we feel or what impression we want to give the people we are talking to.

Sitting in public places and looking at people is the best way to observe how they tend to use their body language to support what they are saying. You can tell that a romantic conversation is taking place between two people, simply by observing their behaviour and facial expressions, which would be completely different from when they are arguing.

We have a natural ability to use our body language together with speech, and no matter how hard we try or even train to hide it, it always remains with us. This natural behaviour can help us learn something about ourselves and use it to communicate more effectively with each other. This is also associated with the way we listen to and observe each other. In a face-to-face conversation we use our vision as well as our hearing, to understand what the other person is saying. We tend to take in a lot of information through our eyes, although speech itself is obviously a powerful communication tool. It is amazing how effective speech can be when supported by visual materials. When both speech and visual elements are appropriately put together, they form a good presentation. The way you combine them determines your presentation style.

The significance of your presentation style

How many times have you attended a presentation where you felt that the presenter was too boring, or too slow? Sometimes it is the complete opposite, the speaker might be entertaining but too fast for you to understand what he or she is talking about.

Try to remember these occasions and any particular aspects of the presentation which made you feel:

- bored or sleepy

- lost

Write down any actions that the speaker could have taken to make you:

- interested

- able to understand.

CREATING YOUR OWN STYLE

It is hard to determine what a good presentation should be like, because various situations require different styles. However, every person has his or her own style and although good presenters can make a slight deviation from the usual, they cannot change it completely. There is a very good reason for that. If you are training yourself to become a presenter, you develop a certain way of speaking, using your body language and, of course, visual aids. All these aspects of the presentation are directly affected by your natural character.

From the choices below, consider the combination which best represents the way you speak:

Speaking speed:	Slow	Medium	Fast
Frequent body movement			
Medium body movement			
No significant body movement			

This should give you a brief summary of your style, only taking two aspects of the way you speak. All you need to do is adjust your natural way of speaking to suit the requirements of the occasions at which you present.

Presentations may involve many figures and diagrams and can be complicated. No matter how simplified the presentation's contents are, the audience can lose interest or miss the point, if the style is not interesting enough to gain their undivided attention. Presentations can be divided into two main categories: formal and informal.

PRESENTING INFORMALLY

Informal presentations range from a progress meeting with the project team or a supervisor, to a two-minute talk with your boss. If you meet your boss in the corridor and he or she asks you the classic question: 'How are things going?', what they really mean is: 'Give us a two-minute presentation on the progress of your work without any details or visual aids.' Because there are no visual aids available to you, you can only use speech and body language.

Remember one occasion where you were faced with the question 'How are things going?'. Which of these reactions did you have?

- highlight issues
- give a short summary of situation
- pause and think
- say 'quite well, thank you'
- panic
- talk for the sake of saying something
- say something you regret saying.

This will show you how you handled the situation.

There isn't one single right way to react to this type of situation, but it is good practice to be brief and only mention the most important points such as the end of a certain task or the time needed to end it and whether everything is going according to the plan. If things are not going so well, it is important to add some reassuring remarks and give a brief description of what you plan to do to solve the problem. If you are looking for a solution, there is no harm in briefly stating the problem. Always be ready for this kind of question and prepare what you want to say in case you get asked to say it.

When conducting a short explanatory conversation with

someone, you need to remember the following points:

- Be as brief as possible.

- Use your body language as your visual aid to help explain your points.

- Be enthusiastic, but not aggressive.

- Choose the key words you want to put across and say them clearly.

- Try not to get too close to the person physically. Some people don't like their space to be invaded.

My boss usually asks me a question, and keeps on walking without giving me the time to summarise the progress of my work. How should I react?
This could be an indication that he or she doesn't really want to know how things are going. In that case, give a short and polite answer. If, however, you feel that you need to talk to them, you can use this opportunity to book some of their time later to discuss matters with them.

Progress meetings
A more detailed type of informal presentation can be a progress meeting, where the supervisor or the project manager wants to be informed about the development of each part of the project. Visual aids can be used in this case if the facilities are available in the meeting room. This is a good opportunity to show your work in a semi-formal way. In order to achieve that, you need to do the following:

- Address your colleagues as you would address them normally. Remember that you are talking to the people you work with every day and not to an audience you are meeting for the first, and probably the last, time.

- Talk about the main points without going into too many details. Time is usually against you.

- Use examples from your daily operations, if applicable.

- Make your presentation interactive, like a two-way conversation.

- Ask the experts to confirm the facts you are stating, when appropriate, especially if the information is relevant to their area of work.

Some traditional presentation techniques – the ones we have drummed into our heads in training classes – may not apply to informal situations. For instance, there is no need to introduce yourself at the beginning. Introducing yourself to your colleagues who know you very well would be, as you may well agree, weird.

Sometimes, saying a few light-hearted remarks can help you to get the message across, because people can remember your points by associating them with jokes that they can easily recall. In presentations aimed at small groups of colleagues, the style can easily be informal, creating a more relaxed environment for the meeting and an opportunity to work without pressure.

Think of six other situations which require an informal presentation style.

PRESENTING FORMALLY

In some situations, it is necessary to give a formal talk to a person or a group of people. This can take place on occasions like sales meetings, public lectures, etc. These are the types of presentation that require careful preparation and a formal style.

Again, there isn't one single right style for formal presentations, but there are some basic aspects of the presentation, to which personal variations can be added, which can be used on different formal occasions. These are listed below.

Dressing appropriately

It is important to be dressed formally and to the standard of the occasion. Wearing your best designer jeans does not count as appropriate. A smart look could help boost your confidence, as well as the audience's confidence in you.

It is advisable to make an effort in finding the right clothes, but do not let it worry you too much and take all your attention. It is there to project a formal image and boost your confidence. Wearing smart clothes also has an effect on the audience because it shows that you respect them and you made the effort to dress appropriately.

Using the right language
Using formal but simple language, with some funny remarks every now and then, is one of the best ways to keep your audience interested, happy, and most importantly, awake. Avoid too many details and too few entertaining remarks, as this will send your audience to sleep. Once you develop the reputation of being a boring presenter, you will find yourself being prescribed as a substitute for sleeping tablets, so be careful.

People are usually tempted to use complicated and very formal words when faced with a formal situation. Try to resist this temptation, as it will confuse you, as well as the listeners, and the talk will eventually become boring. This is particularly true in presentations where the contents can sometimes be hard to follow even when simple language is used.

Using pictures on your slides
Use your slides to tell some of the jokes. A formal slide is not necessarily one which is full of words and complicated sentences. Even politicians joke in their speeches which often wins them applause (do not confuse this with when you may think that the whole speech is a big joke). Funny sketches on your slides may be very effective in driving a point home, as well as entertaining the audience and winning you support.

Introducing yourself
You should begin a formal presentation by introducing yourself, even if most of the audience know you. It is important for everybody to know who you are and, when applicable, who you are representing, which makes them feel more comfortable when listening to you.

Thanking the audience
You should also conclude by thanking everybody for being there and, if applicable, answering any questions they might have.

Think of six occasions where you need a formal style.

TALKING WITH THE RIGHT ATTITUDE

The way you talk is a major contributor to the style of your presentation. Although you should be yourself and talk as you normally do, you may tend to talk in an artificial way when put under pressure. Being yourself under these conditions is easier said than done, in many cases.

In order to reach the required degree of confidence and therefore relaxation, it is necessary to train and prepare yourself before you face the audience. Once the training and rehearsals are completed, you feel more confident to think about what you want to say, as you do not have to worry about the way you say it.

The style in which you present largely depends on the way you talk. Some presenters talk as if they are reading a newspaper, without any emphasis, pauses or body movements. This can grab the audience's attention for a short period but as time goes by, their interest in your presentation will rapidly fade.

From the box below, consider the combination that best describes your style:

	No emphasis	Some emphasis	A lot of emphasis
Pauses only for breath			
Pauses to emphasise			
Many pauses, as speech habit			

Here are a few more suggestions to gain and hold the interest of your audience.

Telling a story

Presenting your ideas in the same way as you would tell a story to a friend is very effective in gaining the audience's undivided attention and trust. Telling a story involves a great deal of enthusiasm and a structured flow of events leading to the conclusion. People enjoy listening to a story being told, whether it is about the new company letterheads or the corporate strategy of the organisation. No matter how boring or complicated the content of your presentation, it becomes more interesting if told as a story.

Speaking with a moderate speed
If you talk too quickly, you may lose the listener. On the other hand, if you are telling your story at a slow pace, you will bore them to death. Moderation is the best option – it keeps the audience interested and looking forward to hearing what is coming next.

Avoiding an artificial accent
Do not worry too much about your accent. If you have a regional accent, or you are presenting in a foreign language, trying to change the way you talk adds to the things you have to think about when presenting, which may confuse you. There is nothing wrong in having an accent which is different from the one your audience have. This, however, may add another reason for you to speak clearly and with a moderate speed, in order to avoid confusing your audience.

SPEAKING WITH YOUR BODY

When you look at people in the street, it is amazing how much you can tell about them by simply observing their body language. It is as if they are transmitting signals by the way they control their facial muscles or move their hands. To prove this to yourself, try the following:

1. Observe people in the park or in other public places.

2. Try to deduce what they are talking about.

3. Draw a conclusion about their character from their body language.

4. Ask a friend to do the same and compare your findings.

This little exercise will prove to you how much you, as well as others, rely on body language to judge characters. When your first contact with a person is over the phone, you tend to form an idea about their personality, judging by their voice. When you meet them face to face, the chances are that your opinion will change according to their looks and body language.

Remember someone who you spoke to on the phone before meeting them face to face. Write down the impression you had of them at the following stages of your relationship:

● on the phone.

● when you met face to face.

● one hour after you met.

Usually people form an impression about you in the first five minutes of your face-to-face meeting. When presenting, an hour is, in most cases, the maximum amount of time you have to keep or change that impression to one that suits you.

When presenting, your body language should reflect a confident, truthful and trustworthy personality, with a good sense of humour. Yes, this does sound like an advert from a dating agency, but it helps you get your message across. In order to achieve that, try the following:

Using your hands

- *Use your hands to invite the audience to accept your point.* This is done by keeping your hands open and your palms pointing upwards. This is more effective if you only use one hand. Remember, you are only inviting them, not begging for forgiveness.

- *Keep your fingers open.* This is particularly valid when you let your hand hang by your side. This position looks more natural.

- *Avoid putting your hand in your pocket.* If you do, you may be tempted to fiddle with loose coins. The interesting rhythms this action generates can be very distracting.

- *Avoid closing your hands firmly.* This projects a protective or aggressive image, which can be the result of lack of confidence.

On the other hand, leaving both your hands dangling loosely, like two dead fish at your sides, may be interpreted as lack of enthusiasm.

- *Avoid holding your hands in front of you or rubbing them.* This forms a protective barrier which separates you from the audience. It is also another way of saying: 'I'm telling you a lie and I'm too scared.'

- *Use a pointer to keep one of your hands busy.* Use it to help the audience focus on specific points on your visual aid.

- *Avoid pointing with one finger at the audience.* Politicians often do this when delivering aggressive speeches, or giving out warnings. Avoiding this is a wise choice, because it can make the audience feel threatened or even offended.

- *Co-ordinate your hand movements with your words.* Whatever you decide to do with your hands, it is very important to time your movements with your words, otherwise they will look mechanical. The movement also has to be relevant to what you are saying. There is nothing more irritating than making a point, then following it with the relevant gesture a few seconds later.

Using your facial expressions and eye contact

When people are looking at you, they tend to focus on your face for most of the time, which makes your facial expressions very important. A smile, from time to time, reassures your audience of your confidence and sincerity. This does not mean you have to keep a tight smile throughout the presentation, like some television show presenters. The following actions can help you use your face effectively:

- *Use your eyebrows* for inviting the observer to accept your ideas.

- *Move your head around and look at people's faces.* This will help you maintain eye contact with them, which is very important. Keeping eye contact with members of the audience makes them feel that you are addressing them personally and that you value their reaction and opinion. If you look at the ceiling or at a piece of paper in front of you, the audience will feel ignored and you will be showing them your lack of confidence.

- *Try not to fix your eyes on one place or person all the time*, as this will isolate the rest of the audience and may be interpreted as lack of confidence on your part. Do not let your eyes wander around. Try to equally divide the time you look at individuals in the audience. It is easy to think of a large audience as one entity and start looking at random, as if you are looking for something or someone you lost.

- *Look at individuals* every time you mention something relevant to the area of their expertise. Of course, this is only possible when you know those people.

- *Look at people even if they may not appear to be looking at you.* The audience, for most of the time, tend to look at the diagrams or pictures being shown behind you if you are using visual aids. This should not prevent you from looking at them, in case they take their eyes off the diagram for a while and expect to see you talking to them, and not to the piece of paper in front of you, or the back wall of the room.

Controlling your movements

In addition to your face and hands, the way you move can also affect your style. Your movements can range from standing in a fixed position, to acting roles which are relevant to your presentation. This depends on the style you want to present in. But as a general rule and a safe option, try the following:

- *Restrict your movements to the necessary.* Some nervous presenters tend to take a few steps back every time they look up at the audience, then move forward when they read from a script or look at the transparency on the overhead project (OHP). This results in a very interesting dance routine which distracts the audience from the content of your presentation.

- *Face the audience, not the board behind you.* If you are using any kind of projection equipment, especially an OHP, it is very important not to keep looking back at the projected image. This is very irritating from the viewpoint of the audience and makes you look nervous. There is no harm in checking whether the projector is in focus and the picture is projected properly at the beginning of the presentation. Once you have done that, however, show your confidence by forgetting about the screen and focusing your attention on the audience.

I find it difficult to stand still when I present. How can I overcome this problem?
This may not necessarily be a problem. In some cases it is natural to move to illustrate an idea or to point at something on the board. If, however, you find yourself moving aimlessly, make a conscious effort to keep your feet in the same position on the floor. Try to find a reference point near you and maintain the same relative position between your feet and that point.

BEING IN CONTROL

By applying the techniques discussed above, you leave little reason for the audience to be irritated or annoyed. It is now time to take a further step and try to keep them interested in your presentation. In order to do that, they must feel relaxed and on top of what is being said. If you are in control of the situation, you can easily achieve that.

This is more about controlling yourself than the audience. Once you are in full control of your actions, you can feel more comfortable in interacting with the audience. The following points may help you achieve that.

- Show your interest in the subject. If you're not interested, why should they be?

- Define the structure of your presentation and be precise.

- Tell jokes which are relevant to the presentation rather than any odd ones.

- Involve the audience by asking specific questions and providing the answers shortly after.

- Be confident.

- Practise to become confident.

Practising
This is the key to a successful presentation. Practice boosts your confidence and helps you stay in control. The more time and effort you spend practising, the less you have to worry when presenting. A

presentation is a live show and you wouldn't go on stage if you hadn't rehearsed enough. Develop a practising technique by trying different methods. Some of these methods are listed below:

- Choose a topic that you feel passionately about and prepare a five minute presentation on it.

- Stand in front of a mirror and present to yourself.

- Repeat this several times, each time observing a different aspect of your style.

- Try to change any habits which contradict the 'rules of the game' described in this chapter.

- Experiment with the various styles and techniques described in this chapter and decide what suits you best.

- Try to film yourself with a video camera if you can.

- Replay the film and observe yourself. This will help you find your mistakes and correct them.

- Get a friend to watch you as you present and give you constructive criticism.

- Do not give up easily. It takes time to change certain habits.

For the above exercises to work effectively, you need to concentrate on the style only. Do not worry about the content of your short presentation – this is not what you should be concerned with at this stage.

After finishing your practice, select three aspects of your style that you were worried about. Think about how you managed to improve or feel more comfortable with them.

I am happy with my style when I practise, but why do I lose control when I face the audience?
To make yourself more comfortable in front of an audience, rehearse your presentation well before giving it. The less you worry

about what you have to say, the more you can concentrate on how you say it. With experience, your presenting style becomes second nature.

CHECKLIST

1. Remember that we communicate by using not only speech but also body language.

2. Be aware of your own natural style of communicating.

3. Be prepared for the casual meeting with your boss in the corridor.

4. Learn how to use jokes appropriately.

5. Dress appropriately for each presentation occasion.

6. Present your ideas as if you were telling a story.

7. Use your hands and facial expressions to enhance your presentation.

8. Control your movements to avoid distracting your audience.

9. Be in control of yourself and of the situation.

10. Practise a presentation in front of a mirror or video camera.

11. Get feedback from a friend.

CASE STUDIES

Fred talks to Joe in the corridor

Fred is a junior member of the marketing team in a medium size company. Being in this position, he ends up being given the tasks that no one else wants to do. He is currently working on filling in a database with customer information and the task may take several weeks. Joe is Fred's manager and he is always busy working on more important tasks, which hardly leaves him enough time to eat his sandwich, let alone having long discussions with Fred. However, he is a very nice man and is prepared to talk with Fred in the corridor, between meetings, to discuss any problems.

Fred and Joe are invited to attend a staff meeting. As Fred is rushing to the meeting room, he meets Joe, who is going to the same place. After greeting each other, Joe asks Fred how his 'data filling' task is going. Enthusiastically, Fred explains how far he still has to go before all the data is entered. He also highlights the fact that the sources of information are becoming limited and there are gaps in the database which might have to remain empty. Joe suggests a contact in a market intelligence agency, who might be able to help in this area.

Lisa leads her team

Lisa manages a small printing company and leads a team of energetic and talented people. She is a very talkative lady who likes to spend her time giving presentations to the team. Her main responsibility seems to be attending as many meetings and exhibitions as possible and, in her spare time, making sure that people who work for her do what they are told to do.

Lisa has scheduled a meeting for Monday morning to be attended by all members of staff. In this meeting, she is giving a presentation on the new contracts awarded to the company and the achievements of the team in the previous week. Everybody arrives at the meeting room on time to listen to what Lisa has to say.

As usual, Lisa is late. After a long wait, she walks into the room and starts the presentation by apologising for not being able to show any slides, because she hasn't had the time to prepare them, ignoring the fact that the company had desktop publishing facilities coming out of their ears and she could have easily prepared a couple of slides. She stands there talking for half an hour, with a very posh accent, using complicated executive language. She does it without giving the chance for anyone to ask a question or give an opinion.

At the end of her shoddy presentation, she asks with a tight smile: 'Any questions?' She pauses for a few seconds and adds: 'Good, let's get out there and do it.'

Mark meets the local residents

Mark manages a housing estate for the local council. He is very good at his job and his team mates are pleased with him. He is a very shy character and he keeps a low profile for as long as he can help it. He realises that his luck has run out, when he has to give a presentation at a residents' meeting to tell them about the refurbishing work which is going to take place over the next year.

Before the meeting, he prepares a short presentation, identifying the main points he wants to put across to the residents. He also jots down a few relevant funny remarks about the estate, like the one about the man who complained to his neighbours about loud music only to realise that it was his daughter producing it in her room.

After the preparations, he rehearses his presentation thoroughly. When he gives the presentation, he is very excited about the new project and its benefits to the local residents, and his enthusiasm is very clear. The residents leave the meeting very happy, looking forward to the next progress meeting.

POINTS TO CONSIDER

1. Who do you think did better in getting their message across and achieving results?

2. How do you think Mark managed to overcome his fear of public speaking?

3. How would you present the progress of your project to your team members, even if they were all working for you?

4. How can you change the aspects of your style that you feel uncomfortable with?

5. How can you keep your audience interested and awake?

6. Neither Lisa nor Fred used any slides. What do you think made Fred's short presentation more effective than Lisa's?

7. What helps you feel more comfortable and in control in front of an audience?

3

Preparing the Presentation Materials

RESEARCHING THE SUBJECT

When faced with the task of giving a presentation to a small or large group of people, the first step you need to take in your preparations is research. Whether you are an expert in the subject or know only a little about it, you need to do some research to come up with the right material for your presentation.

You may, most of the time, know about the subject, but not enough to put an interesting presentation together. In some extreme cases, you may be asked to give a talk on a subject that you do not know much about. In this case, research plays a very important role in the preparation process.

What does researching involve?

The research might involve a number of activities like going to the library, meeting people, watching videos, listening to tapes and reading reports. It also involves knowing who you are going to be presenting to, whether it is your managers, a panel of lecturers or company customers interested in buying your products. The list of possibilities can be endless and it is you who should make a decision on how much background information is needed to make a presentation and sell your ideas to a particular audience.

Asking the basic questions

Before embarking on the task of researching for your presentation, you need to consider the following points, in order to make the right decisions:

- How much do you know about the subject?

- Who are you presenting to?

- For how long are you presenting?

- When and where is the presentation taking place?

Gathering information

Gathering background information may require you to think in a different way on separate occasions. For instance, reading a report or paper requires a different thought process than interviewing someone. Your research may take you to different parts of the country, so you should be prepared for that. You may need to conduct a meeting with a person who works in, say, Manchester and search a database in London, so you have to travel to gather your bits of information.

Gathering information is not an easy task, and you need to put considerable effort into it. The more effort you put in at this stage, the fewer problems you face later. This task may in some cases be daunting, but do not be put off by the magnitude of the task ahead, because it pays off to follow it through.

Identifying sources of information

Treat researching and preparing for a presentation as a small project. Start by identifying the topics you need to cover and work out ways of getting the relevant materials. Find out about the location of each piece of the 'puzzle'. Do you need, say, to talk to an expert in a certain field, to make a few phone calls or to just visit the library on the fourth floor?

Once you know where to find what, it is time to check whether the assumptions you made were correct. Run some checks on the locations of materials involved. Call the library, for instance, to see if the materials are fully or partly held there and if not, try to find out where you can get hold of them.

You are asked to prepare a presentation on the state of schools in your area. Think of five sources of information which can assist you in putting such a presentation together.

Managing your time

As in any project, time management is very important. For good and simple time management, take the following steps:

- Find out how much time you have.

- Work out a schedule.

- Divide the work into small manageable tasks so you keep accurate control over your timetable.

- Draw a plan of action where you correlate the task with its geographical location. Don't book a meeting in, say Glasgow on the same day as a visit to the library in London. The two places are too far away and the task is not easy to accomplish unless you have no limits on your budget.

- List all the activities in a table with the date and estimated time – make sure you leave some buffer time in case you run into trouble.

- Leave an empty column to put a tick next to completed tasks. This helps you see how far down the schedule you are and therefore tells you if you are falling behind.

- List any alternative actions to take if the original plan fails.

- Only put a small amount of information on your plan to avoid confusion. Put any further details on a separate sheet of paper.

This is an example of what a project schedule would look like:

Activity	Date	Time /h	Completed	Alternative
Interview Mr May	08-04			Visit library
Read Document N39	08-04			Talk to John
Talk to Mr James	09-04			Read chapter 5
Video library	09-04			Interview David

Storing your data
It is very nice to be able to collect a large amount of information and data, because it gives you a wider choice for the presentation content. However, if you are overwhelmed by the sheer magnitude of information records, finding a piece of information later can be a difficult task, if not impossible. There are several ways for storing data and these are a few examples:

- File the information and index the files.

- If you have access to a computer database, save the information there and create easy-to-follow search fields. A database does not have to be computerised, it can be held in a well-indexed filing system or a ring binder.

- Some records can't be kept in the same format as the others, e.g. audio tapes of interviews, videos, news cuttings, etc. Keep these under the appropriate indexing system and refer to them in your database.

- Use key search words to classify the information, and divide each file into sub-files. For example, next year's budget can be filed under 'budget' and the 'next year'. This helps you narrow your search down to the exact piece of information you are looking for.

You can choose to use any of the above methods to keep your information in order where you can easily find it later, but never rely on your memory because no matter how good it is, it can easily betray you.

I find it difficult to capture all the information obtained in an interview on paper, especially when it is in the form of comments and jokes.
Don't be afraid to ask the person to clarify or repeat a point. Use a tape recorder if you can to record the interview, then spend some time later producing a paper copy of the conversation which you can file away for future reference.

EXAMPLE: SUMMARISING THE WORK OF A GROUP

Although these methods generally apply to any kind of research, in some cases you need to change your line of action according to the situation and the subject you are going to present. To help illustrate how these methods are put in practice, let us consider an example where a research situation directly related to a presentation is involved.

Picture yourself as a research assistant at a well-known institution. Your department has managed to come up with a consumer product which will improve people's quality of life. You have been asked to give a presentation to a large manufacturer that can help you mass produce your team's invention. You will also need to put a business case together because your presentation is as much about money as it is about the product.

Getting information from your colleagues

The product is the result of a team effort, which means that you have to get as much information as possible from your colleagues about their part of the design, before preparing this presentation. This does not mean that you should obtain every single document involved in the project, as this might take you a very long time to read.

Consider the order of importance of the information sources for each of the three research areas listed below

	Interviews	Documents	Other sources
Financial information	....	....	....
Product details	....	....	....
Selling points/PR policy	....	....	....

In this situation, it is probably best to have short meetings with your colleagues and let them present their parts of the project to you and emphasise the important points that might be of interest to the manufacturer. It is then your job to research these areas and widen your knowledge in them, by paying particular attention to the points emphasised by your colleagues.

It is then time to filter the ideas out, and break them down into categories. This helps you organise your thoughts and provides you with the first building block of your presentation. At this stage you are only collecting materials for your own information, to familiarise yourself with the product's details.

Shopping for ideas

The research stage is similar to shopping. You go to the supermarket to buy the right ingredients to make a soup. You collect everything you need from the shelves and you take them home with you. You may not use all that you bought as ingredients – you may keep some vegetables to use later – which compares to not including all the information you have in your presentation, but at least you know it is there in case you need it.

Filtering the information

Once you feel you have enough ingredients, it is time to decide what quantity you want to use. Putting the presentation together is like cooking. First you have to put in the main ingredients to make the basic dish, then you add salt and spices to make it palatable. The core of the presentation is the information necessary to explain the main features of the product and the financial benefits to the manufacturer. This is only a rough filtering stage to filter out redundant information.

If you have time, check the information again with your colleagues and make sure you understand what they told you. Ask them for their opinion on what you are saying on their behalf. As far as your part of the research is concerned, make sure you go through your documents again to check that you didn't miss anything.

Filling the gaps

At this stage you might feel there are some gaps you can fill in your preparation. You should decide whether it is worth spending more time filling them. This depends on the importance of the missing information as well as the time left for you to prepare for the presentation. If you think you are comfortable with the amount of information you gathered and that you covered all topics to the right extent, it is time to wrap it up. It is very important to know when to stop.

Researching for written reports

Gathering materials for a presentation is very similar to what you do when you write a report. In fact, a presentation is a short oral report. You are reporting your findings to someone using speech and visual aids. Most presentations are accompanied by reports or a written paper, in which case the research is done for writing the report and the presentation would be used only to highlight the important points. If this is the case, you don't need to do a great deal of research for the presentation itself and it is only necessary to think about what to include in it from the report, which takes us to the next building block.

DECIDING ON THE CONTENT

Once you have decided what topics the presentation is going to include, it is important to put it into words that you can remember, or be comfortable with, when you are giving your talk. Getting started is always difficult. To make life easier for yourself, do not start at the beginning. The beginning or introduction is probably the most difficult part to prepare. This is why you should leave it till the end.

Brainstorming
After gathering the information, you become more familiar with the subject you are going to present and ideas start coming to your mind. Write them down without giving any thought to their suitability for the presentation. Ignore the order they should go in. This is a brainstorming session where all the ideas, no matter how important or unimportant, are put on paper at random. During this session, apply the following process:

- Write down the headings of the topics you want to talk about in any place on the paper.

- When you run out of ideas, go back to your research notes to see if you can find some more.

- On a new sheet of paper, group the ideas under separate headings.

- If you can't find a suitable place for an idea, leave it aside for a while. This can help you find a suitable place for it later.

As a brainstorming exercise, work out the subjects that come to your mind if you are preparing to give a talk about your bedroom.

Next, group them under a maximum of five headings.

Aiming for perfection?
Don't try to achieve perfection, because you may never be satisfied with any results and end up spending more time than you anticipated without achieving your goals. However, this should not be an excuse for a poor presentation. Make sure you have some extra time in your schedule for last minute changes, because you might have a new idea after you've written your script and want to move things about.

In many cases, I don't have enough time to do research. How can I have enough information to include in the script?
Use the short time to interview people and ask them to provide you with written material too. In other words, let them help you with the preparation process. Limit the number of points you include in your presentation. It also helps if you spend some time planning, even if your time is limited. This saves you a lot of hassle later and helps you operate more effectively.

WRITING A SCRIPT

Now that you know what to include, it is time to start writing a script for your presentation. You may decide to read that script or memorise it, depending on your skills and abilities. Whatever you choose to do, it is very important to write a script – when you write something down, it is easier for you to find your weaknesses or mistakes and therefore try to correct them. Having a script helps you avoid improvising in your presentation, which is a dangerous risk to take as a presenter, experienced or not.

Remember one of your previous presentations. In the table below, choose the number you believe represents the level of knowledge you had of the subject, the amount of time and effort you spent on preparation and your level of confidence and comfort with the information contained in the presentation, putting aside all the other problems.

Knowledge of the subject	1	2	3			
Level of preparation	1	2	3			
Level of comfort with content	1	2	3	4	5	6

Ideally, your level of comfort with the content of your presentation should be the sum of your level of knowledge of the subject and the level of your preparation.

There is no such thing as the right way to write a script. Script-writing is like politics, where everyone and their dog know best. Choose which way makes you comfortable and use it. You may feel that you know enough about the subject and the topics are well structured in your head so that you only need to sit down for a few minutes and use what your memory can throw together. If this is not the case, you may find the next section very interesting.

The script-writing process
The following is one way of preparing a script which I find effective and simple (see also Figure 2).

Preparing a first draft
- Start developing your ideas into a short story.

- Rely on your memory to start with to see what you can put together without referring to your notes. This helps you clarify your ideas and find out how much you know about the subject off by heart.

- Refer to your notes when you get stuck.

- Try to find any points that you failed to recollect.

- Do not, at this stage, worry about your style or grammar as this will confuse you and delay your thinking process.

Putting the second draft together
The second draft requires a more detailed approach. It is now time to look at the structure of the script and see whether the transition between sections takes place smoothly. If two consecutive ideas are not related, the shift between them becomes noticeable and the presentation loses its continuity. Try to find a link or a point in common with the two ideas and insert it between them.

Apply the following steps when you work on your second draft:

- Put the different sections in the right order to facilitate smooth transition between them.

- Add the right sentences at the beginning and end of each section for a smooth transition.

- Read the script out loud to get a feel of what it sounds like.

Effective language and final changes
After checking the transitions, it is time to divert your attention towards the grammar.

- Make the tone sound formal but do not take it to the extremes as it starts to sound dull. In general, it is more appropriate to use

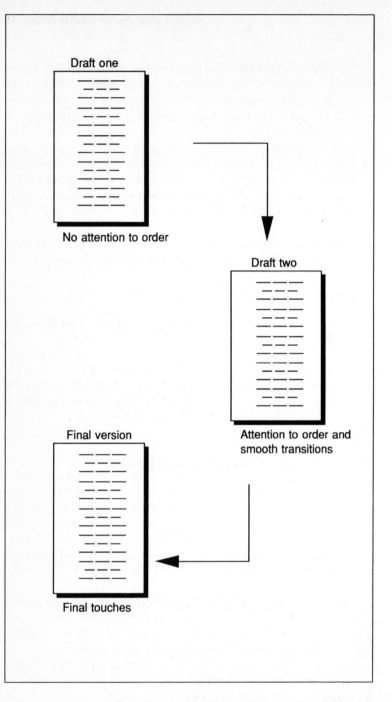

Fig. 2. The script-writing process.

the third person – they, she, his. However, do not hesitate to use the first person – I, we – when appropriate. This also applies to the use of the second person – you. Try not to get carried away with the use of the first person but do not avoid it altogether.

- Avoid expressing yourself in a negative way and use positive terms whenever you can. It is much better to say 'all reasonable offers are accepted' rather than 'no unreasonable offers are refused'. Being positive reflects an inviting image and certainly reduces the possibility of confusion.

- Using factual language reflects a friendly and convincing tone. Extravagant expressions can only help confuse the listener.

- Read your script carefully. Read it again.

- Make any changes that you think can place more emphasis on certain points.

- As you read, start to imagine what diagrams, pictures or charts can be used to support your script. If there is an idea that cannot be supported by visual materials, make it shorter and include it with a closely related topic under one picture.

DEALING WITH EXCESSIVE INFORMATION

An important factor which may affect the length of your script is the time you have. You cannot read a twenty-page script to an audience in three minutes. It is very important that you keep within the time allowed. In order to find out how long it takes you to read your script in a natural way, you need to actually read it and time yourself with a stop-watch. Remember to read it in a conversational tone, with a reasonable speed.

One of the major contributors to the nervous state presenters often find themselves in is running over the allocated time. If you know too much about the subject, or you have done extensive research, you may have a lot to share with your audience.

In the following matrix, place a tick to indicate the combination of information and time allocated, which closely represents most of the situations that you have been in.

		Amount of information		
		Too much	Enough	Too little
Allocated time	Too short			
	Enough			
	Too long			

Ideally, you want to place your tick in the middle of the matrix, but, as you may agree, this is hard to achieve.

Finding a solution

One of the most common problems is to include a large amount of information, within a short time, which can be extremely confusing to your audience. So what is the solution?

If the script is too long, edit it by removing details and leaving highlights of the important points. If removing some details does not solve the problem, it is necessary to get rid of some points altogether. Choose the least crucial points and scrap them. Make sure you leave yourself an extra minute or two to compensate for any unforeseen delays.

What do I do if I am given a long time to present, but do not have enough information to fill that time?

You may not always have to use all the allocated time to pass on a certain amount of information. You can always do some more research to obtain extra knowledge in the subject, or use the remaining time to answer questions or involve the audience with interactive exercises.

The final draft

When all these changes are complete, you will have a final draft of your presentation. It is now up to you to learn it and deliver it as a talk, or to read it to the audience. Whatever you decide to do, try to be as natural as possible when you present it. Now the words are ready, it is time to back them up with some pictures.

CHECKLIST

1. Think about the audience and the context of the presentation before starting your research.

2. Identify possible sources of information.

3. Manage your time effectively.

4. Decide how you will file and store your research findings.

5. Decide what information you will use in the presentation.

6. Always write a script for your presentation.

7. Make sure your script is well-structured and uses appropriate language.

8. Don't try and cram too much information into too short a time.

CASE STUDIES

Nassim gains support

Nassim is a very energetic man involved in many community activities. He works for the local council and always comes up with good ideas for improving the quality of life in his community. One of these ideas is to establish a local information centre with computers connected to the Internet, to be used by students of local schools and local residents as a research facility that puts them in touch with the world. The main challenge he has is that his knowledge of the technical side of the project is that of a monkey about chemistry. The other problem, of course, is money. In order to obtain the support of the local authority and the people and organisations that may be involved, he has to give a presentation outlining his plan.

To learn about the subject and gather as much information as possible, he prepares an action plan listing all the people he needs to interview and the places he has to visit. When he has finished researching the subject, he prepares a presentation script and has the presentation ready. He presents his proposal and many people are impressed, especially those who have negative ideas about the Internet simply because they don't know much about it.

Samantha gives advice

Samantha never fails to give a very interesting and entertaining presentation. Well, at least that's what she thinks (and so does her boyfriend). She works in a careers centre in a well-known university. She is asked to give a presentation to final-year biology students on the employability of graduates in this subject. She has all the information she needs and it isn't too difficult to obtain all the information from her reliable resources. She has half an hour to give the presentation and answer questions. She prepares a script, putting in it all the information she has. Because she is too excited about the subject, she manages to talk for forty minutes and then offers to answer questions after she has put most of the audience to sleep.

Helen presents at school

Helen is a fire officer. She is asked by a local school to give a talk to young students about fire hazards as the Fifth of November is approaching. She assumes that the target audience is teenagers and prepares a presentation accordingly, with a well-structured script and a video made specifically for this kind of presentation and designed to address teenagers. When she turns up on the day, she is taken to a classroom full of drawings of yellow dinosaurs and pink elephants and six-year-old children eager to listen to her. A simple question to the head teacher could have saved her time, effort and embarrassment.

POINTS TO CONSIDER

1. What made Nassim's research effective?

2. All three characters in the case studies prepared a script. What made Nassim's script more effective than the others?

3. Why is preparing a research action plan so important?

4. How can following the script-writing process described in this chapter help you prepare a winning presentation?

5. Why do you think it is important not to use more time than allocated for your presentation?

4

Planning Your Talk

DRAWING A PRESENTATION LAYOUT

This is your chance to be an artist, if you are not one already. It is an opportunity to put your imagination to the test and see what it can come up with. You now have to sit down and group your words under separate frames. No matter what kind of visual materials and aids you use, you have to create frames within which you put your ideas and sentences.

Putting your ideas in the right sequence

Your ideas can be arranged in several ways, depending on who you are presenting to and what you want to put across. You have three main choices:

- Start with the least important statement and end with a very important finding, building up to a spectacular ending. This is particularly effective if you are presenting to a hostile audience that you expect to disagree with you. You start by stating your ideas and gradually convince them, before you declare your final proposal.

- Start by stating your suggestion, or your punch line, if you are presenting to a friendly audience. You can then go into more details to explain your decision.

- Take the audience through a journey. This is particularly effective when you are presenting the different progress phases of a project, or the development of a certain scheme from day one.

It is essential to know who your audience are and follow the steps described in Figure 3.

How can I structure my talk if I don't know what reaction to expect from the audience?
Always be on the safe side. Do not start with a very controversial

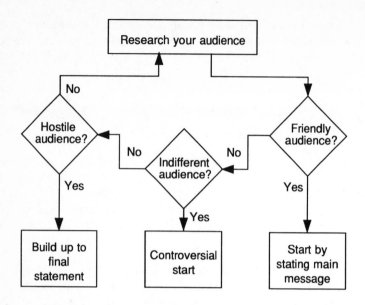

Fig. 3. The right sequence.

statement. Keep some extra ideas up your sleeve and analyse the feedback from the audience (body language, answers to your questions, etc.) and throw in a few more suggestions if your audience do not appear to be hostile.

The contents of your slides

If you are using visual aids, particularly transparencies or slides, you need to make sure that what goes on them ties up with what you put in your script.

From now on, the term 'slide' will be used to refer to 35 mm slides, transparencies or any frame within which visual aid materials are presented. A slide can be shown on a transparency, a computer monitor or any other means of image projection.

Deciding how many slides you need for a presentation is a difficult matter. Depending on the length of your presentation, you define the time for which you can project a slide. As a general rule, a good time would be 5 to 10 per cent of the total presentation time or about 2 minutes, whichever is shorter. Otherwise the time would be too short for people to absorb the information, or too long, so it gets boring.

Think of the type of slides you usually produce. Place a tick in the matrix below, indicating the closest combination to your normal slide contents. Do that for the one slide that best represents your style.

	Diagrams	Words	Cartoons
Words			
Diagrams			
Cartoons			

Use the following suggestions when deciding on the content of your slides:

1. *Put the least possible information on one slide.* There is nothing more confusing than an overcrowded screen. Some presenters tend to put pictures, text and diagrams on one transparency to save themselves the hassle of making another one or two. This forces them to keep the slide projected for too long which may make life easier for them but much harder for the audience. Remember, the harder you make it on yourself, the easier it is for the audience to understand your ideas.

2. *The content of the slide should be directly related to what you are saying*, in which case you can point at parts of it, as you go along, to direct the audience's attention to some important points. Don't be afraid to include funny pictures or cartoons in a formal or technical presentation. There is nothing wrong with that – unless you only use cartoons and nothing else which turns your presentation into a comedy show.

3. *Think about your audience* when you are deciding what to include in your slide. Will they prefer pictures and block diagrams rather than equations and tables? Is it a good idea to include a graph to illustrate a particular point? The answers to these questions lie in the audience. If you know what they want, you can base your presentation on it. As a general guide, it is good practice to avoid writing equations unless extremely necessary. Use graphs to talk

about test results or statistics. Charts are also very effective in showing your findings.

4. *In technical presentations,* it is more effective to use block diagrams and simplified flow charts to explain the various parts of the system or the process stages.

5. *Consider alternatives to the conventional way* of representing figures or classifying things. Instead of using a bar chart to represent, for instance, the number of people interested in the product, you can use 'ghost' or 'matchstick' people on top of each other (vertically) or holding hands next to each other.

6. *Do not be tempted to photocopy pages from your report* and put them on a transparency, to save yourself some work. If you need to copy a diagram or graph, fine, but don't copy any text with it. Things like the page number, or the end of a paragraph, are irrelevant to what you are showing; they distract the audience and make your presentation look shoddy.

What quality should you aim for?

Being creative does not mean you have to be Michaelangelo. You don't need to draw perfect pictures. People want to understand what you are saying and are not interested in the quality of the pictures you are showing. A drawing is used to help illustrate a point and not as part of an art exhibition. However, you should take some time to draw any pictures in the final stage and make use of a computer package if available. Take some time to finalise your pictures and give them a more professional look.

Now that you know what should and should not go on a slide, you need to go back to the drawing board to make a presentation layout before embarking on the task of producing the final slides.

Combining text with slides

A presentation is, in a way, a public performance and should be treated like a short theatre or film production. To help you decide what slide should accompany each part of your speech, you need to do a **treatment** or a **story board**.

A **treatment** is when you divide your script into small sections and write them one under the other, perhaps in a tabulated form. You then write a description of the accompanying slide next to each section.

Treatment

Text	*Slide contents*
.... It is essential for you to update your skills to join the wave of change and keep up with the changes in things surrounding us.	Man surfing and reading a book Title: Keeping up with the changes
....Computers are becoming an essential tool in modern communications and in everyday life. Struggling with them will be a constant struggle with modern life.	Man fighting computer Title: Struggling with modern life

... It is essential for you to update your skills to join the wave of change and keep up with the changes in things surrounding us.

Keeping up with the changes

... Computers are becoming an essential tool in modern communications and in everyday life. Struggling with them will be a constant struggle with modern life.

Struggling with modern life

OW! YOU'RE SUPPOSED TO BE USER FRIENDLY!

Fig. 4. Story board.

A **story board** can be clearer and more easily understood. You may know what you want to have there but it is difficult for other people to guess it. You may by now be asking what other people have to do with all this. Well, you may ask someone else to prepare the slides for you. Having a story board can also help you remember the pictures if you are likely to forget what you mean by the descriptions above.

In a story board, you draw the picture to go on the slide opposite the piece of script that you want it to go with (see Figure 4). If you are not good at drawing, never mind. Rough pictures, 'matchstick' or 'ghost' people are good enough at this stage. You can write notes under the pictures if it is not possible to include some details in the frame.

> Produce a five-slide story board for a short presentation on the benefits of frozen pizza (the type that you find in supermarket refrigerators). Think of what kind of pictures can support your arguments and imprint themselves in the mind of your audience.

How can I produce professional looking slides, if I don't have a computer-based drawing package, let alone time?
Make it very simple. Use a ruler and colour markers to draw on transparencies. Use simple drawings and geometrical shapes, e.g. matchstick people, triangles, etc. You can always use a flip chart or a board to reinforce the argument or drive a point home. But most importantly, keep it simple and avoid messy drawings.

WHAT TO SAY AND WHEN TO SAY IT

In earlier chapters we have looked at how to structure your presentation and use the appropriate style for different occasions. It is time to take another step and learn a few tricks which help you produce a smooth and effective presentation. In your script, you should phrase your ideas in a way that convinces the audience. In other words, you should know what to say and when to say it.

The introduction
If you enter the room without anyone formally introducing you to the audience, it is necessary to say your name, affiliation – if you are not presenting to your colleagues, and a brief description or the title

of what you are going to talk about. You can start by saying: 'Good afternoon ladies and gentlemen, I am (name) from (your affiliation) and am here to present (the subject of your presentation).'

If, however, you were introduced by someone else or you are very well known to the audience, you can start in a different way. Consider first the mood your audience is likely to be in. Take the appropriate action for each of the following attitudes of the audience:

1. *Waiting for you to start.* There is no need to capture their attention, start when you are ready.

2. *Expected to disagree with your proposals or ideas.* Don't make matters worse by starting with an announcement that can only help stir the situation. If you are suggesting, say, a revolutionary departmental restructuring and you expect many people to oppose you, don't start by simply suggesting the idea. If you do so, you would encourage them to block you off and stop listening to you, depriving you of the chance to explain yourself.

3. *Indifferent audience.* For this type of audience, you need to be controversial. Start with something which provokes their interest and forces them to listen to you.

After assessing the mood of the audience, depending on who is going to be present, you have to decide on the type of opening to use. There are several kinds of introduction for the situations described above, and here are some of the tried and most effective openings:

- Start straight by involving the audience through questions that will make them think about the subject you are presenting. 'Good morning. Were you ever caught in the traffic and wished you could contact the office to know the outcome of a certain meeting? If your answer is yes, I'd like you to sit comfortably and let me introduce you to the best way to keep in touch with the world.' This can be the opening of a presentation about a newly designed mobile phone or a portable fax machine, for example.

- Start with an unexpected statement to seize the audience's attention. You can say, for example: 'Investing in a portable phone is a waste of money. That's what cable companies keep saying...' Don't forget to pause for a second or so after the statement before backing it up with an explanation.

- Thank the person who introduced you, if he or she is known to the audience. Also thank the organisers of the event or the people who invited you to give a presentation. 'I would like to thank the board for giving me the opportunity to present my findings and to say how pleased I am to be here today.'

Use these examples as a brief guide and choose the right words for the right situation. It is important to memorise the opening lines because the most difficult part of a presentation is the opening.

Explaining the body of your presentation
The audience is now listening to you and waiting for you to start, after you managed to capture their undivided attention. You are telling your audience a story, and it is important to repeat the main points, throughout the presentation, for them to remember.

After your introduction, you tell them what you are going to tell them in the coming few minutes. Do that in the following steps:

1. Start by saying a few words about the contents of the presentation. Mention the most important points and don't cram the slide with headings of the various sections of your script. Avoid using too many words especially on the first slide.

2. Later in your presentation, give them a reminder of what you said. 'This is how far the technology has advanced over the last two years. What is then happening with the European market?' This will provide you with a reminder of what you said as well as a smooth transition between the technology and the European market. At the end of the presentation, a final reminder will ensure that everybody remembers what you said.

3. Bear in mind that people can only concentrate for ten to fifteen minutes. Keep them interested by timing your funny remarks to coincide with the audience's weak moments. Don't spoil your joke by letting them know that you are going to tell one. Make sure your jokes are highly relevant, and don't bring in any old story just for the sake of being funny, as people will start wondering about its relevance.

4. Another way of getting people's attention back is to ask them direct questions. 'If you are faced with this choice, which component would you use?' If you notice that someone is on the verge of sleeping, you can look at them as you say these words. They will think you are asking them a direct question. This will wake them up and keep them awake for a while. Direct audience involvement and colourful visual aids are other ways of seizing the audience's attention. These methods are discussed in Chapters 5 and 7.

Choosing your closing words

Your last words, in the presentation that is, have to be remembered by the audience. The conclusion is your chance to achieve this. It certainly is not the place to introduce new ideas. Your conclusion may cover things related to the introduction and the content of the presentation such as what course of action was taken, or what could have been achieved if more time was invested, and what further investigations can be done in the future.

Think hard about what thoughts you want the audience to leave the room with. Don't be afraid of being slightly poetic in the last few words, after telling the audience 'what you've told them.' A last sentence could be: 'This model makes use of the latest technology to provide an invaluable service and put you in touch with the world wherever you are.' After this you can say that you would be glad and do your best to answer any questions.

SELLING YOUR IDEAS

The purpose of most presentations is to explain ideas and convince people that the concepts being presented are true and of benefit to them. In order to do this, you need to use an effective language which makes an impact on your audience. Many of the effective techniques were discussed previously in this chapter. However, to take things one step further and add a more professional touch to your presentation, you need to know a few more effective ways of leaving an impression on people.

More effective tricks

The use of short and clear sentences makes it easier for the audience to understand your ideas. Once they understand them, it becomes easier for them to be convinced. Two main points that you always need to remember:

1. Use expressions that are familiar to the audience.

2. Avoid using words that can mean different things to different people.

Rhetorical tricks are widely used by public speakers and some comedians. If you listen to them carefully, you will undoubtedly notice their existence in the speech. They work for presentations too, helping you increase your chances of persuading people with your ideas. The most important are:

- contrasts

- repetitions

- lists of three.

Here is an example where all three tricks are combined together, trying to convince the council members to fund a cost effective local community centre:

> 'If you think that not having a community centre contributes to the increase in youth problems – this is the solution...
> If you think providing a centre for the community causes financial problems – this is the solution...
> And if you think a youth centre will make our community a better place to live in – then support our centre, because it will...'

Notice the contrast in the first two suggestions and the corresponding replies. Both suggestions include the word 'problem' and both replies have the word 'solution' in them.

The repetition of 'if you think' is obvious and acts as a common point between the three ideas. In the first two replies, 'this is the solution' is also a repetition, emphasising the fact that the community care centre is offering all the solutions to the main problems. The use of the same technique of 'problem followed by solution' also counts as a repetition.

Finally, the list of three builds up to a spectacular ending. It deals with three different thoughts that the audience might have. It increases your chances of putting the right ideas across by providing you with three chances to get it right.

These tricks usually draw applause from the audience for public speeches or laughs for comedians. Used in a presentation, they help you convince the audience more effectively. Instead of applauding, they would agree with you and become more receptive to any other ideas you may have.

> Think of three sentences, or words, that would help you sell a new vacuum cleaner. Include features of your choice.

The right wording
Your presentation script should include words that you use when you talk. It is not a news programme that you are presenting. You are conducting a friendly talk with the audience. Think of the audience as customers to whom you are selling ideas or products.

The way you phrase your words is extremely important. A small change in a sentence can decide the outcome of your presentation. Using 'Don't you think...' is better than 'I think...' while 'from the facts you have seen and your experience and knowledge in the field, you can deduce that...' is preferable to 'I'm going to show you how these findings prove...'.

'You probably haven't considered this option' may intimidate the audience because you are suggesting that they are ignorant. Remember that people like to feel well informed and the use of 'I'm sure you are aware of...' will be very helpful in suggesting that.

Helpful points to remember
When choosing the right wording to convey a message, consider the following points:

- *Avoid the use of unnecessary words* which only help you to stall for time. These are words and sentences like:

> 'May I draw your attention to...'
> 'The other point I want to discuss'
> 'To explain this in another way...'
> 'More or less...'

- *Make a conscious effort not to use 'time filling sounds'* like 'em's and 'er's. For a typical example of the use of these sounds listen to your average aircraft pilot: 'This is your pilot speaking, we er... are approaching our er... destination. If you look out of the windows on the er... your left, you will er... see...' If you can't think of something to say, don't feel obliged to fill the time. A silent pause can help you regroup your ideas and give a breather to the audience.

- *Explain any acronyms* before you use them and remind people of their meaning every now and then. TCS can mean Total Customer Satisfaction to you but to others it might mean Traveller's Cheques Sales.

- *Phrase your ideas in the form of questions* and, when possible, in a way which invites the listener to agree. Make the questions simple with a yes or no answer. 'Is this the right choice?' – pause, then provide your version of the answer without saying that you are going to do so. 'The use of this fluid in the cooling system will provide a safe way of....' During the pause, the audience had the time to think about the answer. This makes them more receptive to what you suggest later.

- *Avoid generating resistance or arguments* by imposing certain ideas. People in general do not feel comfortable with being told what to think or do.

- *Arouse people's personal interests* by mentioning things directly related to them. If you know the interests of people in the audience you can include them in the talk. 'As an expert in the field, Mr Smith would be the first person to agree that a 5 per cent increase in the price will redefine our market position....' This will make Mr Smith proud of himself and you. But make sure that your suggestion is correct and have an argument ready to back it up.

FITTING THE CONTENTS WITHIN THE TIME

Everything you say or do is directly affected by the number of minutes or seconds you have. One of the biggest worries for presenters is overrunning. Careful preparation saves you the panic that running over time can cause.

I have seen people prepare for their presentation without giving any consideration to the time they have, then they try to squeeze all the information in the space of a few minutes. You should be guided by the time allowed for you to speak and decide what to say accordingly.

The time you have can be dictated by the circumstances. You may be one of ten people to present on the same day and therefore given fifteen minutes for your presentation. On other occasions, you may have the choice of how long you want to present for. Don't be tempted to talk for a long time. The shorter the presentation, the more impact it has on the audience. Remember, people tend to lose concentration as time goes by.

Allocating the time

When you are allocating the given time to the different sections of the presentation, remember the following:

1. Do not include too many details. This is very difficult in many presentations. A person who has spent a whole year working on a project may find it very difficult to present it in ten minutes.

2. Find out which points are relevant to the requirements of your audience. Only include those in your presentation. There is no need to say that an engine is capable of operating in sub-zero temperatures if you know it is going to be operating in a desert.

3. Say the truth and nothing but the truth but not necessarily the whole truth, as this may take a very long time. Try to make your presentation short by not including unnecessary details. Anything that doesn't sell or convince should be left out.

Longer presentations are for major works and conferences, where experts are willing to listen to specific details about a certain discovery or invention. It is then appropriate to go into details, because the audience has the same level of knowledge and interest in the subject as yourself. A long presentation can take the form of a lecture too.

Sometimes, the total allocated time for your presentation includes the time for taking questions at the end. Decide for how long you are prepared to take questions and exclude it from your time allocation. Don't be tempted to use some of this time to overrun with your presentation. Answering questions is a very important part of presenting.

Making effective use of time

When you decide or find out for how long you are going to speak, time yourself during rehearsals and cut out the unnecessary bits that make you overrun. A common mistake is to read the script while you time yourself. You usually read at a different speed from when you talk. Instead of just reading, deliver your presentation as if you had an audience, including all the pauses and with your normal speed of talking. Make sure you finish a minute or so before the allocated time as you tend to be slower sometimes under real conditions.

Here are some suggestions to help you stick to your schedule and use your time effectively:

- During the presentation, put a watch – preferably with digital display – somewhere you can see it. Look at it from time to time to see how long you have left and control your speed accordingly, without letting the audience notice because that can be irritating. If you find this confusing, try to develop the ability to tell for how long you have been speaking without looking at your watch. This can be achieved with experience or training.

- Choose a paragraph from a book, read it with your normal talking speed and time yourself. Do the same for another equally long paragraph. Repeat the same procedure for longer paragraphs and try to guess the length of time you have been speaking for. Doing this several times will help you find out how long it takes you to say a given number of words.

- Another method is to make your script fit the time and then roughly memorise your words. This will enable you to stop exactly on time, without having to worry about it.

- If your visual aids require some time to switch from one slide to another, try to include them in your rehearsals. If they are not available at the time of preparation, take them into account and allow another minute or so for changing slides.

- Present on your own several times and time yourself. Adjust the speed of your talk each time to make it fit comfortably within the given time. If it doesn't, go back to the drawing board and take out a few sentences or ideas.

BACKING UP YOUR MEMORY

There are three different ways of delivering a talk:

- remembering the content
- reading from a script
- using notes.

You can use any of these three methods depending on your abilities, the time you have to prepare for the presentation and your knowledge of the subject you are presenting.

Which of the above methods do you use for each of the following levels of knowledge in a certain subject:

	Memory	Script	Notes
Little knowledge	....	....	....
Adequate knowledge	....	....	....
Expert	....	....	....

You may find that you usually use a different method in each situation, which is a very normal thing to do. However, it is often easier to use a mixture of two methods – memory and notes is a very popular combination.

Remembering your script

The memory method is the most natural and effective. If you know a great deal about the subject, you can read your script, rehearse presenting it several times and remember key points or, if you can, all of it. You may need to write down important figures or references on a small card as memory back-up in case you fail to remember them.

This technique can be very effective if you can deliver your talk in a natural way without letting the audience sense that you are trying to remember your lines. To sound natural, be spontaneous and comment on things in the room or events taking place on the day, relating them to the contents of your presentation when you can. You can always prepare these remarks shortly before the start of your presentation.

Reading your script

This is the safest option. If you don't have enough time to memorise your script, or feel that your memory is not good enough to hold all the necessary information, then this is your best bet. This is also a safe option for avoiding mistakes.

Although it is safer to read from a script, you have to be skilled. The script can sometimes act as a barrier between you and the audience. You can easily get carried away and stop looking at the audience for long periods. To keep eye contact while reading from a script, some public speakers, especially politicians, use reflective glass in front of them, to reflect their queued script from a television monitor, without the audience seeing the reflection. This is not very practical in ordinary presentations.

When reading from a script, you have to be able to pause when necessary and remember when to use the right gestures. Some people like to write stage directions to remind them when to pause, change tone or make a certain gesture. This may become confusing if too many directions are included. If you're not able to adopt a conversational tone and maintain eye contact with the audience, you're better off using notes.

Using notes

If you know the subject reasonably well, it is enough to make notes on cards not exceeding the size of a postcard.

If you decide to use notes, remember the following:

- The notes should include the main points of your presentation as well as some reminders if required. These are words like 'pause, check the time' or even self-encouragements like 'you are doing well' or 'go for it'. These remarks can help boost your confidence.

- Use small, stiff note cards for easy handling.

- Your notes should be as short as possible. Write headings and the points you want to make about them. Keep refining your notes as you prepare for the presentation.

- Keep the cards handy when rehearsing so you can highlight the points that you think are very important and are likely to forget. Remember that the notes are only to help you remember your script. It is still important to write a script and make a 'story board' when possible.

- Don't be tempted to use more notes than you need, as this will confuse you. If you can attach your cards together by punching holes in them and tying them together, you avoid mixing them up. Only refer to your notes when you need them. Remember, they are there to help your memory, not to act as a substitute for a script.

I never have enough space on my note cards to fit the contents of my presentation. How can I overcome that obstacle?
This is simple. Remember that these are note cards and not script papers. Only put the major headings and ideas on them and remember the rest. When you see yourself writing bits and pieces of script which you probably find difficult to remember, stop and keep what goes on the card strictly under control.

Using your slides
Another way of remembering key points and the order in which you want to maintain them, is to rely on your slides. By looking at the contents of the slide, if you are using an overhead projector, you can see the points listed in front of you. Only use this method when you know your subject very well and you have rehearsed your presentation several times together with the visual aids.

Having the important facts at hand
Have all the important facts, that you have or haven't mentioned in the presentation, written down on a piece of paper that you put somewhere near you. This will be useful when asked a certain question that you cannot answer without referring to your figures or research findings.

Choosing the right method
Always choose the method you are most comfortable with to deliver your presentation. Don't push yourself too hard to remember things. If you can't remember your script, use an alternative method. Whichever option you decide to take, talk as naturally as you can and be confident. After all, this is a chance for you to show other people what you can offer them, so take the opportunity to express yourself in the way you feel more comfortable with.

CHECKLIST

1. The way you sequence your ideas depends on the subject and the type of audience.

2. If you are using visual aids such as slides, make sure they tie in well with your script.

3. Your style of introduction will depend on the context and the mood of the audience.

4. In the main body of the presentation, repeat the main points to ensure your audience can remember them.

5. Choose your closing words carefully as you will want the audience to remember them.

6. Learn to use 'rhetorical tricks' naturally and easily.

7. Practise the presentation several times to ensure it fits the given time.

8. Decide whether you are going to remember the content, read from a script, or use notes.

CASE STUDIES

Gill uses her artistic talents

Gill is responsible for resource allocation in a hospital. She basically looks into the availability of beds for patients who use the hospital. She has looked at the numbers of patients over the last few years and the operations scheduled for the coming year and has developed an effective method of making the right resources available.

To present this method to her superiors, she decides to replace all the charts and numbers in her presentation with diagrams and cartoons. She uses her artistic talent, which is limited, to draw matchstick people and basic geometrical shapes, and produces a story board. Then she makes use of a basic drawing package on her personal computer to produce the transparencies. Her presentation is well received.

Simon fails to time himself

Simon is a university lecturer. He is asked to give a special lecture before the Christmas break to a large audience of lecturers and students from different departments. He is given one hour for the lecture and taking questions. The lecture is on his speciality subject.

On the day, he puts his digital watch in front of him to keep track of time, but forgets to look at it. He gets carried away in his talk, constantly drifting from his prepared script. The lecture is fascinating to begin with, then it starts to get boring. He then realises that he only has a few minutes left. He starts rushing to finish the talk and mention the remaining points. He finishes with one minute to spare for taking the twenty or so interesting and valuable questions at the end.

Alice uses note cards

Alice works in the security department. She is asked to give a presentation on the new security measures following a computer equipment burglary in the building. She has a problem remembering her script, so she decides to write the main points on note cards.

She is very familiar with the new security measures because she helped put them together herself. Her only weakness is that she can't remember the sequence of topics she wants to discuss in her presentation. The note cards prompt her at the right times.

POINTS TO CONSIDER

1. How would you structure your presentation to address an audience expected to disagree with your ideas?

2. What advantages does a story board offer you over a treatment?

3. How could Simon have improved on his timing?

4. If you decide to use note cards for memory back-up, what would you write on them?

5

Preparing Visual Aids

ENHANCING YOUR PRESENTATION

Visual aids are used to help you drive your points home. They also offer your audience a visual representation of your thoughts. It is much easier to express yourself with the use of pictures, graphs and models. You can explain a point much faster if you use pictures. This will enable the audience to understand your point and remember it.

Try a simple experiment to see how effective using pictures is, compared with the use of words only. For this you need the help of a friend. Draw a picture of a house with a cloud over it, without letting your friend see it. You then both sit back to back, with your friend holding a pen and paper ready to draw what you describe. Try to describe the picture to the other person, without mentioning the words 'cloud' or 'house'.

This will be a difficult task but a very funny one, especially when you look at his or her version of the cloud and the house. It would have been much easier for both of you, if you had shown your friend the picture. You will also notice that you start making gestures with your hands even though you know your friend is not looking at you. If you make the rules of the game even harder by not allowing any hand movements, you soon notice you are trying to move your head.

By now, you will have realised the importance of using pictures to help illustrate a point. They by no means replace words altogether, but they help clarify your ideas and save you the trouble of explaining concepts or designs with words only. Although you may be able to express yourself without visual aids, will the audience fully absorb and remember what you are explaining in a short period of time?

Capturing your audience

Can you imagine road signs without pictures? How long would it take you to read 'give priority to vehicles from opposite direction'? Would it not be much faster to see the sign associated with this action? There is no way you can match the effect of the symbols and colour codes with words on their own.

Visual aids also play the role of keeping the audience interested in the presentation as well as helping you to deliver an effective message. They achieve that in the following ways:

- By changing the scene from time to time, a new interest is created for the people watching. By the time they fully explore what's on the screen, you give them a new picture to look at.

- If you are an inexperienced presenter, or feel nervous in front of audiences, visual aids draw people's attention away from you. This will help you relax and concentrate on your talk. If you are nervous, visual aids help you divert your apparent signs of panic by simply handling them.

You can deduce from all this, that visual aids form a very important part of a good presentation. Combined with words, they help you communicate ideas in a very short time and leave a long-lasting impression on the audience. This, however, is only true if you use them properly, otherwise they might do the opposite.

USING PICTURES TO DELIVER YOUR MESSAGE

Visual aids are not effective if they are not carefully prepared to include, as in the script, the important points that are vital to convince the audience. The way these points are presented is also important. Both the content and the presentation of a slide contribute to the impact it has on the viewers.

The contents

Cram too much information on one slide and you're guaranteed to confuse your audience. Whether you use graphs, pictures or diagrams to explain an idea, put only one of these on one slide. The contents should be directly related to the corresponding script.

Choose from the table below, the number which best represents the proportions of your various slide contents. Choose one number from each row and add the total of the chosen numbers for each column.

	Diagrams	Pictures	Words
Little	1	1	1
Half	2	2	2
Over half	3	3	3
Total			

Ideally, the three totals should add up to a maximum of four for one slide.

A good clear slide consists of a heading and a body. The heading is usually written with big letters and tells us, in brief, what is presented in the slide. 'Operating Plan Forecast' is a suitable heading for a slide showing a graph with the operating figures plotted against time.

The body is where you put the materials you want to present. You can combine pictures with words and figures. When working on the body of a slide, keep the following points in mind:

- Remember KISS (Keep It Short and Simple).

- Use pictures whenever you can and keep the number of words and figures to a minimum (see Figure 5).

- Leave plenty of space between items for clear visibility. If the viewer has to make an effort to see or understand what's on the slide it is better to change it.

- Your pictures do not have to be drawn perfectly, but it is good practice to draw clear images to provide a professional look to your presentation. If you can get the help of an artist or a computer package for drawing pictures your slides will be clear and professional.

Throughout the presentation, try to use the same style for all your slides. If one slide contains your company logo, for instance, all the other ones should have it too. Try to keep the background items the

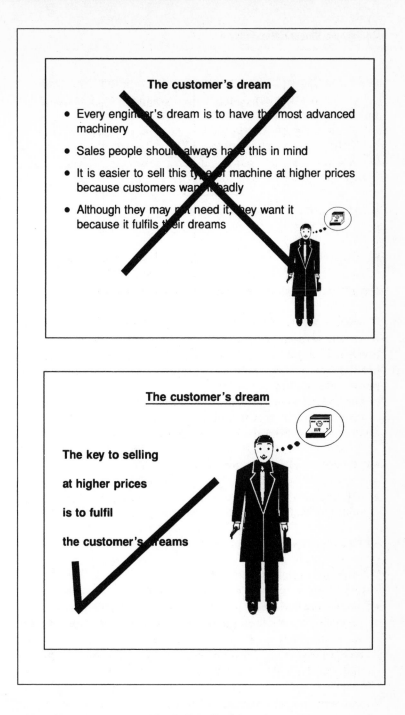

Fig. 5. Sample slides.

same in all slides. This will give your presentation a professional appearance and is better than having slides that look as if they came from different places.

You can change the background items and colour if you want to use an element of shock. Switching from blue to yellow provides a big jump in the picture and therefore surprises the audience. Don't use this too often as it may lose its effect.

Sometimes I find it difficult to get the right picture that describes my thoughts and find myself writing words on the slide. Is this wrong?

No, it isn't wrong. You can put words only on some of your slides, as long as there are not too many. Don't just read the words off the slide. Only use brief headings and elucidate them in your talk.

Presenting with visual aids
Visual aids are there to help you, not to cause you problems. You should be comfortable with using the equipment in order to divert the attention of the audience away from you and towards the contents of your presentation. Remember the following when presenting with visual aids:

- Ignore the existence of a picture behind you unless you are pointing at it. Don't turn your back to the audience. Can you imagine a weather presenter with his or her back to the camera? What would your feelings be in this situation?

- Always rehearse with your visual aids. This will help you familiarise yourself with the equipment and remember the order in which the slides are going to be projected.

- If you are using an overhead projector, make sure that all your acetates are in order. Put them back in the same order when you finish so you can find them later when answering questions. Use a ring binder to avoid losing your transparencies or mixing them up.

- Do not cover half of your transparency if you don't want the audience to see what is coming next. Use two separate sheets instead.

- Stand to one side of the overhead projector and hold the pointer with the hand nearest to it. This will enable you to use the other hand freely. Let the pointer touch the points you want to draw attention to. Your hand may be shivering slightly due to nervous energy and if the pointer isn't touching any surface, the movement will be apparent to the audience. This is particularly apparent when a laser pointer is used.

- Don't point aimlessly at your slide. Be specific and only point at the section you are talking about. Move your pointer to illustrate any movements in a diagram. The flow of liquid in a system, for example, can be simulated by moving the pointer across the diagram in the direction of the flow.

Tools for visual aids

Visual aids consist of slides and the equipment required to project or show them. Some are very commonly used in presentations and others are less popular due to the difficulties associated with using them or their rare existence in most places. Here is a list of various visual aids and their uses:

Using an overhead projector (OHP)
This is the most popular of all visual aids. It is widely used in all forms of presentations because of its great flexibility. You can use it to project virtually any kind of material, including maps, pictures, graphs and diagrams. You don't need a dark room for it.

Another advantage is that it enables you to see the contents of your transparency and point at it while facing the audience. Seeing the slide helps you remember the points you want to talk about. You can also let your pointer rest on the transparency concealing any shivering of your hand which can be magnified by the projector's lens.

You can lay acetates on top of each other to reveal more information on parts of a chart, for example. Don't be tempted to mask sections of your transparency and reveal them when the time is right. Some people think this is a good idea, but I don't agree. It may make it easier for you to explain a point, but it is frustrating for the audience. Use the former method, if you like, to add more information to the screen.

Using a slide projector
This is the second most popular way of presenting visual materials. It gives a formal look to your visual materials and is particularly effective when used with large audiences.

The quality of the projected picture is very good, as long as it is used in a dark room. A drawback is that you need to point at the projected picture itself which may force you to turn round a bit.

Before starting your presentation, make sure that all the slides are placed in the right order and more importantly the right way up. There is nothing more embarrassing than projecting an image up-side down – apart from walking into the room without any clothes on.

Using a monitor view panel or a data projector
This is a new method of projection. The device has a transparent liquid crystal display (LCD) screen which, when connected to a computer, acts as a monitor. The LCD screen can then be placed on an OHP to replace an acetate. You can use a computer presentation package to display your slides. A variation of this is the data projector which has a built-in light bulb. This eliminates the need for an OHD.

This method has the same drawbacks as the slide projector as it only operates in a darkened room. However, it has the advantages of an OHP as far as pointing and seeing the picture is concerned. You can look at the computer monitor to see your slide and use the cursor in the computer's software package to point at any part of the picture. This, obviously, requires a software package on your personal computer (PC) to prepare and drive the presentation.

Using a video
This is the most effective visual aid of all. However, it should only be used for a short time during the presentation to show something which may be difficult to illustrate using conventional methods. It can also provide more information than speech and slides, in the same length of time.

You can show an extract from a film or make your own video if you have the facilities. This involves computer software, a video camera and editing facilities. You can make moving images to effectively drive a point home. Look in your local *Yellow Pages* for promotion video producers if you want your video to be produced by professionals.

If you can afford to invest in making a professional video specially for your presentation, it can be worthwhile. However, don't let it take over from you, it is only a short and effective visual aid and not the whole presentation.

Using a video can add some complication to the preparation procedure. You have to make sure that the monitor is available and working properly. If you are presenting in a large hall with a video projector, you have to make sure that it is operational before you start your presentation.

Using other visual aids
Having decided on what to use as the main method for projecting your slides, you can use other ways to illustrate some points during the presentation, or to help you in answering questions afterwards. The following methods usually go down well with small audiences.

● *The flip chart.* This enables you to draw a picture or write down formulae and equations. If you are letting the audience participate by answering questions, or making guesses, you can write what they say on the board. It is equally acceptable to use an empty acetate on the OHP.

● *Models and prototypes.* There is nothing better than showing the actual thing. A product prototype shown to the audience or even passed among them is worth a thousand words. Displaying models of buildings can be more effective than showing plans.

● *Demonstrations of prototypes* are effective but can easily go wrong. Make sure that your prototype works perfectly and if you're not 100 per cent sure, you're better off not demonstrating it. Can you imagine how embarrassing it is trying to sell something that doesn't work? Although the fault may be due to something trivial, it doesn't look good in a live demonstration.

ADDING COLOUR FOR GREATER IMPACT

Colour is a powerful way to make important information stand out. By using colour, you can add a great deal of emphasis to certain ideas. It adds a professional, finished touch to visual materials. Attention is gained by striking colours and long-lasting impacts on the audience are made. You can hide messages in colour. You may use red, for instance, to indicate a warning as in traffic signals.

The audience can focus on the coloured parts with the background information remaining the background. Using colour increases the effect of visual aids on the viewer. Imagine a presentation in black and white. For how long can you maintain your concentration? Using colour makes the presentation more

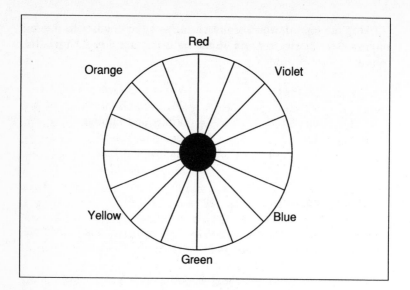

Fig. 6. The colour wheel.

lively and keeps the audience interested. In order to use colour effectively, it is necessary to know more about it.

What is colour?

We all know what the word 'colour' means, so there is no point in being philosophical and trying to define it. However, it is necessary to appreciate the way different colours are combined to produce an infinite range of possible shades for each main colour.

Colour is something we see. It is the reflected light wavelength that varies in different materials to make us see a different colour. Sometimes placing three different colours very close to each other results in a fourth colour if looked at from a distance.

We can identify six different main colours – excluding black and white. They can be placed in a circle according to their relationship. This circle is called the 'colour wheel' (see Figure 6). It starts with red at the top then goes through violet, blue, green, yellow, orange and back to red. Between any two colours there are a large number of different hues.

By varying the lightness or darkness of one colour, we can gradually move towards the next one. For example, orange is a dark form of yellow and a light form of red. From this relationship, it is possible to identify the colours that go well together and avoid using the ones that are completely unrelated.

Using the colour wheel, connect each of the colours in the left column with the two colours on the right that are a slight variation from it:

Orange	Violet and Green
Yellow	Orange and Green
Green	Violet and Orange
Blue	Red and Yellow
Violet	Yellow and Blue
Red	Green and Blue

Combining colours

If two opposing colours like red and green are placed next to each other, they distract the eye and make the viewer feel uncomfortable. However, if you choose to use this combination, vary the darkness of both colours to achieve harmony.

To achieve harmony in colour as well as the right level of impact on the audience, remember the following tips:

- Two hues near to each other, such as red and orange or blue and violet, can be used to achieve harmony. They provide a relaxing combination for the viewer's eye. If they touch each other, they do not tend to 'vibrate' because the area or line in common between them is a hue of both colours.

- To create a contrast between two ideas, or make a point stand out from the background colour, select two hues with three colours between them on the colour wheel. For instance, light orange contrasts very well with red and so does dark green with yellow. Always use brighter colours in the foreground for maximum impact.

- Black and white are also two important colours that should not be completely ignored. Planning the use of black and white should be a part of your strategy to use colour. Black usually goes well with bright colours and white with dark hues.

Making effective use of colour

Playing with colour can be a tricky business. It involves taste, and different people have different ideas about matters involving their personal opinion. You should carefully plan and control your use of colour to give the right impression. Here is a list of do's and don'ts to assist you in making decisions about using colour.

- Use colour in a way which is consistent with accepted conventions when possible. For instance, red can be used for rejection while green indicates safety.

- Don't use colour simply to decorate as you may risk losing its effect. Remember, it is there as an extra tool to help you explain, so use it for this purpose only.

- Establish a certain pattern and keep to it throughout your presentation. This creates a sense of expectancy for the audience. Break the consistency when you want to emphasise a point. If you show your audience something they're not expecting to see, they will notice it.

- Use one colour for similar items to show their relation to each other. This is particularly effective in charts where you can use colour as an extra axis. Don't forget to provide a legend for colour and meaning.

- Don't use too many colours in a small space. If you have to include several colours to differentiate between items of one picture or chart, make sure you make them large enough to be clearly visible by the audience. Space them out and use thick lines to help the viewers discriminate between different sections.

- Make slides with dark background for light rooms and use light background colours for darker rooms. The projected image tends to be lighter than the one on the transparency or the computer screen, so take that into account too.

- For bright colours, use darker backgrounds for a greater effect.

- In graphs, if you have many lines, avoid colouring them in different colours. This confuses the audience. Only colour the one you want to emphasise. If you are giving a computer driven presentation, you can build the slide by adding the lines one at a time, dimming the previous line as the new coloured one appears.

- Use solid, high contrast colours and lines with large enough font sizes to be seen from the back of the room or hall.

WORKING WITH COMPUTERS

Computers are now increasingly playing a very important role in presentations. Whether in making or presenting slides, the results look more professional and effective with the use of presentation or graphics software.

Creating slides

Using a drawing package can be enough to produce impressive diagrams with colours. This method may take a lot of time and effort, because you have to draw your own pictures. A more professional approach is to use a presentation package. This may contain ready made pictures, professionally drawn by experts, for you to use.

Some presentation packages can produce different kinds of transitions between slides. This makes them suitable for use in 'on screen presentations' where the slides are shown directly on the computer monitor. In addition, a presentation video can be much more effective with moving images produced by various transitions between slides.

With the computer facilities, slides can be transferred on to any presentation medium, such as transparencies or small projection slides. Using a scanner can provide you with an extra facility. You can scan diagrams or pictures into your computer, enhance them using the necessary software and use them as part of your presentation.

You can check your spelling with some presentation software packages. This is, however, no substitute for your own checking. The software cannot spot all the mistakes. For instance, 'sending a massage by post' is perfectly acceptable to a software spell check.

Giving on screen presentations

On screen presentations are when you display your slides straight from your computer screen, using data projection equipment. For this you can use a 'monitor view panel', which is described earlier in this chapter, or a data projector. Data projectors are now very popular and can be bought or hired. Make sure you test the view panel together with your slide and adjust the colours before starting your presentation.

For effective use of animated presentations using computers, follow these guidelines:

- Check the speed of transition between any two slides and adjust it according to the speed of your computer when connected to the view panel or data projector.

- Try to incorporate a logical transition which follows on from the previous one. If, for instance, you wipe from left to right, use a similar wipe in the next slide. This sets expectations and when you depart from this consistency, you provide an element of surprise to emphasise a certain point.

- Build slides gradually. You can do that with most presentation software packages. Various sections of the slide can be added gradually at the push of a button. Sections that appeared previously can be dimmed to make the new ones more prominent.

- In some presentation packages you can add animations, sounds and video clips. Make sure you don't overdo it with multimedia presentations.

- Links to other presentation files, documents or even web pages can also be made. Refer to the help menu on your software package for details on how to create them.

- Some older versions of view panels tend to heat up after long use, so make sure you don't switch them on until you want to start your presentation.

- If in doubt refer to the equipment and software manuals for tips on how to use them effectively.

Using colour and computer screens

Using colour with computers can be a tricky business. What you see on the screen is not what you print on the transparency or what you project on the view panel. Check that the colours you are using can be displayed properly on the view panel before your presentation. Similarly, make sure that the printed colours are what you want before you design all the slides.

Computer screens use Red, Green and Blue (RGB) to specify colour. Different combinations and intensities of these colours result in the appearance of many different hues and colours on the screen. Three phosphors exist in each pixel of the computer monitor to represent the three RGB colours.

Each phosphor can produce up to 256 light intensities. By varying these intensities, nearly 16 million different colours can be obtained depending on the colour monitor and the video card used in the system. A black phosphor can be obtained by simply switching it off. A green, red and black phosphor combination, for example, results in a yellow pixel. Magenta is produced by combining red, black and blue phosphors.

View panels
Monitor view panels are a monitor in their own right. If the capacity of your computer monitor to produce colour is different from that of the view panel, your colours will be different when projected. They will also be fainter than the originals, because of the nature of the liquid crystal display.

Printed slides
Your printer may use a different way of producing colour. By combining cyan, yellow and magenta, several colour combinations can be obtained. This method will produce similar colours to those on your screen. How similar, depends on the software application you are using. Keep in mind that colours appear faint when projected from a transparency, so make sure you use dark hues for printing on acetate.

Scanned colours
If you are scanning colour pictures from reports or other sources, don't expect to see a perfect reproduction of the original colours on your computer monitor. This is because colour values on your computer are different from the ones on the scanner. The same scanner can produce different colours on different computers. Use your software application to edit the colours in order to obtain the best results. Refer to your scanner, printer and application manuals for best colour printing results.

If you have a computer presentation package, try to print well defined colours on your colour printer. Observe the difference. Now try to print more complicated shades and hues. How similar are they to the picture on your screen?

The idea of a computer driven presentation interests me, but I'm not familiar with the presentation packages. How can I get to know about them?
The first step is to obtain more information about what they can do

by contacting computer software suppliers. If you are interested, it might be a good idea to invest in a package and learn how to use it by reading the manual. If you want to learn more quickly, it is possible to book yourself on a training course for a specific package.

What do I do if I don't have a colour printer?
There is nothing wrong with monochrome slides. You can still use pictures and shades of grey and black to emphasise points. Remember that black and white are two important and effective colours.

CHOOSING THE RIGHT EQUIPMENT

It is important to use the right kind of visual aids for each occasion. If used incorrectly, visual aids can give the wrong message or even ruin the chances of success in explaining to the audience certain concepts.

Choosing the right visual aid is a difficult task which can be made easier if certain points are considered. Here is a list of things to think about when deciding what visual aid to use:

1. *The ability to grab the audience's attention.* There is no point in using the most impressive high-tech equipment if it won't appeal to the audience.

2. *The size of the equipment.* Your visual aids should be large enough to be seen by all the members of the audience. It is no good using a small television monitor to show a video in a large lecture theatre.

3. *The suitability for the occasion.* You don't need to use state of the art projection techniques if you are giving a short progress presentation to your supervisor. On the other hand, if you are giving a large annual lecture on an important occasion, it is advisable to put some effort into producing and presenting your visual materials.

4. *The effect of your visual aids on the audience.* Ask yourself the question: will it really help explain the point or is it going to confuse the audience or distract them from the main idea? Some presenters use two OHPs in an attempt to impress the audience.

They put, say, a block diagram on one and a detailed schematic of some parts on the other. The viewers in this case can't decide which screen to look at.

5. *The availability of equipment.* Don't count on using a slide projector if the room only has an OHP. Make sure that what you need will be available.

You can also think about an effective way to show any prototypes or models. If they are too small, like a camera lens mounted on a microchip, for example, you should pass it to the audience to inspect rather than put it on a table next to you where it might look like an ant.

Think back to four different situations where you had to present. What type of visual aid did you use? What type do you think you should have used, now that you have read this section of the book?

USING NOTES AND HANDOUTS

It is useful sometimes to provide the audience with something to refer to during the presentation in case they miss a certain point. Giving out handouts or notes containing scaled versions of your slides together with some additional information can help deliver the message (see Figure 7). Only provide handouts when needed and not at the start of the presentation.

Handouts
Handouts can be produced in some computer packages where you can fit more than one slide on an A4 size paper. Diagrams, the details of which can be forgotten once the corresponding transparency is removed, can be included for the audience to refer to.

Notes
Notes can also be distributed to the audience to refer to after the presentation is over. These should include details and figures that may or may not be mentioned in the presentation. They should also be planned carefully and produced in the form of a small report.

A certain training organisation provides delegates with copies of course slides. I have collected many of them but now I find it difficult to understand the content because no notes are attached.

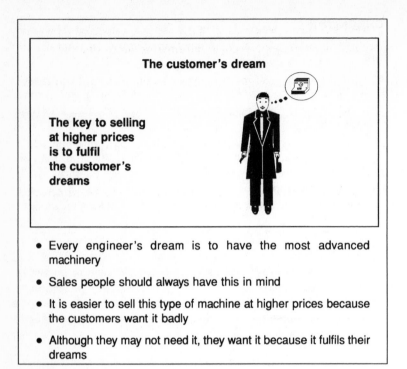

Fig. 7. Sample note page.

INVOLVING YOUR AUDIENCE

Sometimes, you may choose to involve the audience in an interactive presentation. If you need to make a quick survey or opinion poll to prove a certain point, you can pass a short questionnaire to the audience and get someone to help you in counting the votes while you are presenting. Use this if necessary to prove a point and not just for the sake of impressing people with an interactive presentation, because they simply won't be impressed.

Two final tips

Always remember, visual aids are there to help you and if they don't you're better off without them.

Make a few extra slides to assist you in answering questions after your presentation. Don't hesitate to use them – people like to see an enthusiastic presenter who's prepared for everything.

CHECKLIST

1. Don't try to cram too much information on to one slide.

2. Make sure you are comfortable using your visual aid equipment.

3. Use colour for additional impact.

4. Learn which colour combinations achieve harmony and which create effective contrasts.

5. Computer software packages can produce more professional slides.

6. Choose the right kind of visual aids for each occasion.

7. Careful use of notes and handouts will increase the impact of your presentation.

8. Always remember that visual aids should help you, not make life more difficult.

CASE STUDIES

Robert sells his design

Robert is a talented architect. He enters a competition to design a new exhibition centre in the capital, overlooking the river, and is asked to give a presentation about his design to a panel of judges. He prepares a well-structured presentation and creates reasonable slides according to the instructions provided by the sponsors. His competitors prepare their presentations which are also very good. Robert's advantage is that he brings with him a model of his proposed design, which is not mentioned in the instructions, and asks the panel to inspect it and ask any questions that come to their mind. This helps him a lot and he wins the competition.

Fiona gets famous

Fiona works in a large department store and is the resident fashion expert. She is asked to give a presentation on the new collection for the coming year. Fiona, being a professional woman, decides to prepare a presentation on 35 mm slides. She gets all the slides drawn, including on each of them a photo of the fashion item, a list of the selling points and a graph of the expected demand by the customers in the coming year.

Fiona leads a very busy life, so she takes her work home with her. In the evening, she arranges the slides in the right order and puts them in the special box that goes in the slide projector.

The following day, while everybody is struggling to read the small print on the crowded slides and keep up with Fiona's speed, a picture of her posing on a beach in Spain suddenly appears on the screen. 'I'm really sorry, I don't know how this one got in here,' says Fiona with a blush on her face.

Nadia makes effective use of colour

Nadia works in a government department, responsible for funding large engineering projects for the public sector. She is working on the development of a scheme in which private organisations can contribute to the development of public projects. She invites a group of departmental managers to attend one of her presentations on the subject, in order to review her scheme.

Her plan is to compare the advantages and disadvantages of such a proposal, and try to show that the positive points can take over in importance from the negative ones. She is in favour of the private contribution ideas and therefore uses orange graphs on a dark blue background to show the long-term benefits of the scheme. For the public funding points, she uses a lower contrast. When she superimposes the two graphs, the one that she wants to draw the audience's attention to, that is the private funding graph, looks more prominent.

POINTS TO CONSIDER

1. How would you distribute the use of diagrams, pictures and words on one slide?

2. Which visual aid tools would you use for the following occasions: (a) a presentation to your colleagues, (b) a formal talk in a conference, and (c) a presentation to a medium-size audience of business customers?

3. What were Fiona's two mistakes?

4. What other method could Nadia have used to achieve the same result?

6

Speaking Effectively

DELIVERING THE MESSAGE

Statistics show that *what* you say accounts for only about 7 per c
of the overall effect of your presentation, while 38 per cent
accounted for by the *way* you say it. Using the right voice to g
your talk together with the right body language can make a
difference to the effectiveness of your presentation in delivering
right message.

This does not justify ignoring the contents of your presentati
That 7 per cent can make all the difference between convinc
people of your ideas or failing to do so. However, the way you deli
your presentation is of vital importance.

Speaking better depends on several factors such as body langu
preparation of the contents of the speech and the voice. For
effective presentation most, if not all, of the audience's senses sho
be involved:

(a) they see you and what's on the slides
(b) they can participate in a demonstration by touching or smell
    something
(c) they certainly listen to you.

Thinking about voices

The voice plays a very important role in a presentation – it can k
people interested or send them to sleep. Can you think of a lectu
who has a monotone voice that uses the same pitch with no life
movement in it? Can you also remember how close to sleep
became during his or her lectures? I bet you can. In fact you
remember how boring the lecturer was but you can hardly remem
what he or she was saying.

Voice is a powerful tool when used effectively in a presentation (
speech. Think about great speakers, those who left an impact on y
life, and think about their voices and the way they controlled the

In order to develop an interesting voice, let us see how it works.

KNOWING YOUR VOICE

Voice is the result of air coming out of the lungs causing the vocal chords to vibrate producing various sounds. These sounds are shaped into words by the speech organs in the head.

The brain sends messages controlling the breathing and the tension of the vocal chords. These are folds of flesh with gaps between them, through which air can travel making sounds, similar to playing a wind pipe.

This process is also similar to playing a guitar, where the same string can produce different sounds depending on how loose or tight it is. However, this is not the whole story. These sounds need to be amplified in order to be projected out of the body. Like a guitar, cavities in the body, such as the mouth and the chest, provide the required amplification.

The amplified sounds are then shaped into recognisable speech by the tongue, lips, teeth and so on. Speech is produced in two different ways:

1. *Voiced sounds*: produced by speech organs in the mouth closer to the vocal chords at the back end of the tongue. The sound of the letter K is produced in this way.

2. *Unvoiced sounds*: produced mainly using the tongue and front teeth. The sound of the letter S is produced in this way.

All the above aspects of voice and speech are controlled by body organs that are unique to each person. We can develop the ability to control these organs to produce the speech quality that we want. This can be achieved by training the various muscles that produce and shape sounds. The shape of various cavities, such as the chest, can be changed to vary the level of sound amplification.

DEVELOPING AN INTERESTING VOICE

It is possible to identify and improve on four characteristics of your speech: **tone**, **pitch**, **volume** and **clarity**. You can analyse and identify the weak points in them in order to improve them.

Tone

An empty wine glass produces a tone when hit by a fork. A half full, or half empty, glass produces a different tone from an empty one. Try this experiment with two glasses and listen to the difference in tones. You will notice that the tone produced by the empty glass has more resonance and body.

Your voice works in the same way. If you constrict your body cavities responsible for amplifying sound, your voice will sound restricted and sometimes nasal. Restricting body cavities can happen by standing or sitting in the wrong way.

Pitch

Have you ever tried to make music with an elastic band? It is quite simple: stretch the elastic band between your teeth and one of your hands. With the other hand, hit the band using one of your finger nails. If you start stretching and loosening the band, you will hear sounds with different pitches.

The same happens to your voice chords as you stretch and loosen them. When stretched, the number of vibrations increases due to the small distance allowed for them to vibrate. These vibrations produce high frequency (pitch) sounds. When the vocal chords are loose, more distance is allowed for them to vibrate which makes them produce low frequency (pitch) sounds.

Volume

The volume can be increased in two different ways. The first is by increasing the pressure of air coming out of your lungs, or by narrowing the space between the vocal chords (glottis). You can change the volume of a whisper simply by increasing the amount of air through your glottis which is widely open. Try to shout; you will notice that your glottis contracts sharply, to increase the volume of your voice.

Clarity

To get your message across you need to say it clearly. Try to imagine how you would sound if you spoke loudly and got most of your words incomplete because of the lack of clarity.

Clarity is determined by the speech organs and how well you can control them. If you are too nervous your tongue and lips start playing tricks on you because they are tense. You realise that you have difficulties in pronouncing letters like 'l' and 'm'.

In order to speak clearly, overcome the problems associated with speech organs and get your message across, remember the following:

- Exercise your speech organs by consciously controlling every move of your tongue when you are saying a difficult word. If you find this difficult when speaking fast, slow down. After a while you will find that this will become your natural way of speaking.

- Don't be scared of moving your lips. Remember that it might help the listener if they see the shape of a particular sound on your face. For example, rounded lips are associated with the letter 'o' and if a person can't hear the sound properly, at least they can see it on your face. If you exercise your speech muscles it becomes easier for you to control them together with other muscles in your face which will also help your facial expressions be more accurate and expressive.

- If you are presenting in a foreign language, it is very important to pronounce clearly and speak more slowly than normal, especially if you have a strong accent. Speaking clearly helps you surmount the accent obstacle and deliver your message to the audience.

Have you ever been to an international conference where speakers from different nationalities were giving talks in foreign languages? Do you remember a presentation where it was only half way through that you realised it was actually in English? I certainly do.

CAPTURING THE AUDIENCE WITH YOUR VOICE

To capture the audience's attention, is to keep them interested in your presentation. An interesting voice is simply a voice that keeps the listener interested. People agree on the principle and know that it is common sense. However, some people find it difficult to have such a voice. What may sound interesting for you could be extremely boring for the audience.

Finding the right pitch

People in general feel more comfortable listening to a smooth and deep voice. Sometimes they feel comfortable enough to go to sleep. Don't try to force the pitch of your voice lower than its normal limit as this will make you sound artificial.

On the other hand, there is nothing worse than stretching your voice to a much higher pitch than its natural one. Speakers tend to do that at the beginning of their speeches because of tension caused by being nervous or over excited.

You will sound very natural if you speak around your natural pitch. You still need to vary your pitch up and down to sound more lively and less boring. Speaking at the same pitch for a long time without any variations can be disastrous.

To find your **natural pitch**, if you are not already a singer, do the following:

1. Speak at the lowest note that feels comfortable to you.

2. Use a musical instrument, such as a guitar or a piano, and find the note that corresponds to your lowest comfortable pitch.

3. Move four notes up the musical scale. This should be very close to your natural pitch.

4. Try to tune your voice with this note and speak with the music helping you to stay in tune.

5. Practise this as many times as you need, in order to become confident in finding your natural pitch fairly quickly.

Now that you have found your natural pitch you can add some **variations** to your speech to make it more natural, lively and interesting. Changing the pitch up and down according to the contents of the speech helps you keep the audience attracted to what you are saying and also awake. If you think that you can't do that naturally and without straining your speech organs, try a little exercise.

Say the following sentences out loud, as if you were talking to someone normally, and notice the way you say them:

- I'm afraid I have some bad news.

- Congratulations! You've won a big prize!

- Don't you ever talk to me like that again.

You can notice the relation between the contents of the sentences and your pitch when saying each of them. Now that you have realised what you are capable of doing with your voice, you can start consciously varying the pitch. Try this little exercise. Say out loud:

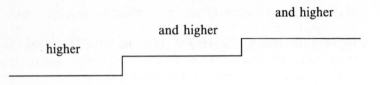

As you say it, change the pitch of your voice to go higher as you say each word. Now try saying:

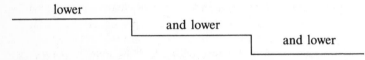

bringing your pitch down with each word. Keep the volume of your voice constant during the exercise.

Singing also helps you realise the potential of your voice organs. If you sing occasionally, your ability to vary your pitch increases. Reading out loud and trying to act out the story with your voice can also help you develop the ability to control your pitch naturally.

USING SILENCE AND PAUSES EFFECTIVELY

Sometimes, silence can be more effective than words. Many presenters feel compelled to fill the silence because they are too scared of it. They end up using sounds like 'emm' or words like 'well'.

It is useful to pause from time to time to allow the listeners to absorb the idea you have put across. A short pause may feel like a very long time to you but to the audience it is a chance to think about what you have said or to wake up if they are sleeping. If you use a video camera to film yourself presenting, you realise that pauses which felt like decades for you were only for one or two seconds.

You can also use the pauses to relax and breathe. Pauses also help you put your ideas together to start elaborating on a new point. For rapid speakers, pauses are essential for their breathing and recharging. There is nothing wrong in speaking rapidly as long as the breathing is regular and the articulation is clear.

Here are some usuful hints on the use of pauses:

- Don't feel compelled to fill the silence. If you find yourself speaking quickly with no apparent reason, force yourself to pause. Sometimes you may be very enthusiastic about what you are saying and find yourself speaking rapidly. Pause and use your body language and voice to show your enthusiasm.

- Avoid becoming a slow speaker. Moderate the speed of your talk to the level of its contents. Always remember that the aim is to be understood and not to say as many words as possible within the given time or to fill the whole time with words.

- Try to maintain the rhythm and the rate of flow of ideas throughout your presentation. Again, this can be achieved by practising your presentation enough times to make you feel confident and in command.

USING STRESS AND EMPHASIS

Pauses are not the only way to emphasise a certain point or idea. The amount of stress put on a syllable can also emphasise the word. Say the following sentences putting the emphasis on the word in *italic* each time.

- Would you give me the *book* please?

- Would you give *me* the book please?

In the first sentence you are asking for the book and not something else. In the second version, you want the book to be given to you, rather than someone else. Although it is exactly the same sentence, placing the stress on a different word can change the whole meaning.

This can be used to emphasise a point in your presentation. If you want to emphasise the time-scale of a certain project you are presenting, you can say:

'It took *two years* to develop this medicine at the cost of $1 million.'

If, however, you want to direct the attention of your audience towards the cost of the project, you might say the same sentence in a different way:

> 'It took two years to develop this medicine at the cost of $1 *million*.'

Avoid putting emphasis on every other word. This diminishes the effect of this technique and renders it useless. Look at the following passage first with the emphasis as shown. Try to change the emphasis to other words and notice the effect. Use this as a practice exercise.

> 'The advances in digital technology are such that by the year 2010 a silicon chip that has the same processing power as a human brain *will* be developed. Programming this chip is going to be *very* expensive. This will *force* the television, computer and telecommunications industries to merge creating a *large* application for this chip which will provide sufficient funds to pay for the costly software required.'

Think about the message this paragraph is trying to put across. Can you alter the message by changing the emphasis to other words?

Changing pitch
One way is to vary the pitch going up and then down at the end of the word or series of words, e.g. 'The design was based on the *latest technology* available.' This makes the word or sentence sound important. Words can also be emphasised by putting some anger in them and saying them decisively, e.g. 'This is the *only way* to do it.'

Speaking decisively
It is also important to realise that emphasis in many cases is placed on a group of words rather than just one. The same technique applies, but in the case of a group of words, the pitch change or the decisive tone can be extended to include all the words in the group. The whole group should be treated as one entity with the emphasis on the group and not individual words.

Applying these techniques
Use the pauses and emphases effectively and spread them thoughout your presentation. A pause right after an emphasis can have a

double effect. Try to use the emphasis with the pitch change more often than the decisive tone to avoid coming across as aggressive.

PROJECTING YOUR VOICE WITHOUT LOSING IT

Have your ever been to a theatre with no sound system and were able to hear the actors clearly? I certainly have. Actors can make you hear even a whisper from a distance. This proves that voice can be projected without an increase in the volume.

Voice projection depends on two main factors:

1. physical

2. psychological.

The physical factor comprises:

(a) the force with which you breathe

(b) the muscular power you put into forming the words

(c) the clarity of your pronunciation.

If you get all these factors right, you will have no problem in projecting your voice. But this is only half the story.

Some people feel nervous in front of audiences and they fail to project their voice properly. In some cases, speakers project their voice too much or too little simply because they do not look at the audience and estimate the power they need to project. I often find people projecting their voice in a small room as if they were addressing a large audience in a 600-seat conference hall. This can be due to nervous energy channelling itself through the voice.

Estimating the projection needed

In order to estimate the projection power required for a specific audience or room, look at the person the furthest away from you and imagine you are talking to him or her. Psychologically you will feel the need to project your voice towards that person and you will be able to control your vocal organs and breathing accordingly.

Practising the technique

Try the following exercise, recording your voice using a good quality tape recorder:

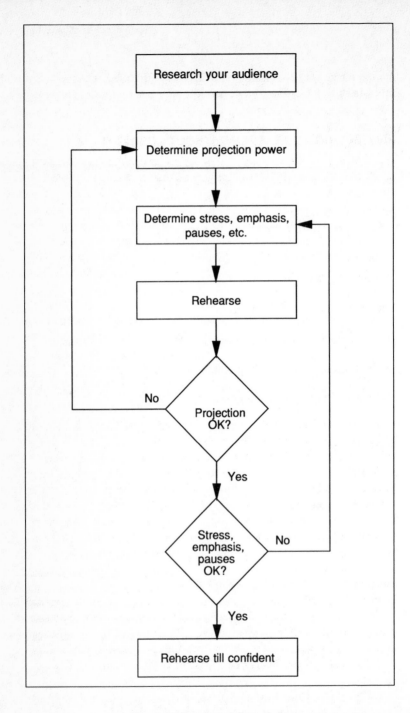

Fig. 8. Voice control flow chart.

Imagine that you are talking to a group of five people sitting in the same room with you and say: 'I am not projecting my voice too far' as you would say it normally, without having to project your voice.

Now look out of the window and focus on an object or building at a considerable distance and say: 'I am now projecting my voice as far as I can' as if you are talking to someone near that object or building.

Throughout the exercise try to keep the same volume. If you find it hard to keep a constant volume, use your hand to remind you. Stretch your hand in front of you and move it sideways as you speak keeping it at the same level. If you do this exercise enough times you will be able to control your voice projection. (See also Figure 8.)

Using your body

To help you project your voice, you can make use of the resonance of your body cavities. To achieve maximum resonance, try the following steps:

- Relax the muscles in your neck and stand comfortably without bending or over-straightening your chest.

- Also relax the muscles in your neck by nodding gently a few times.

- Take a deep breath and exhale, letting out a deep sound. You can then realise how the cavity in your chest resonates giving out a sigh of relief.

Relaxing your tongue and jaws

The tongue and jaws should also be relaxed. Tense muscles in that area reduce the space for resonance in the mouth. **Relax your tongue** by stretching it out of your mouth and pointing its tip towards your chin. Say 'too' several times letting your tongue touch your lower teeth. Stretch your tongue out of your mouth and move it sideways.

To **relax your jaws**, stroke them gently with your hand and relax the muscles until they drop gently. Hold your chin with your hand and wiggle your jaw up and down relying completely on your hand movement and not the muscles of your jaws. Yawning can also help relax the muscles in your mouth. Don't move your jaws sideways as this does not help to relax the muscles.

When your mouth muscles are relaxed they will provide more space for resonance and your voice will be projected further. Letting your body resonate naturally as you speak helps you project your voice without too much effort.

Thinking about your nose

A clear nose also helps you speak clearly and project your voice. If your nose is blocked, it is harder for you to pronounce certain letters let alone project your voice. It is also easier to breathe through a clear nose and therefore maintain the breathing rhythm.

Avoid speaking with a nasal voice. This is when you allow too much air to escape from your nose when pronouncing words. All letters that you can pronounce when your nose is blocked should not be pronounced through the nose anyway.

Try blocking your nose with your fingers and say the letter 'E'. A vowel should be pronounced through the throat not the nose. Try the same experiment with other vowels and work on pronouncing them through your throat rather than your nose. This does not apply to vowels only – other letters can be pronounced in the same way too. Experiment with the alphabet and identify which letters should be pronounced through the nose and which should rely on the throat.

Improving your posture

Other cavities in the body, such as the chest, can be used to create more resonance. It helps if your posture is right. For a good posture, try the following:

- Relax your muscles especially around the shoulder area. To do so you need to raise your shoulders and drop them a few times. You will find after doing it that your shoulders will take their natural position.

- Do not bend forward as you speak. This prevents your chest cavity from resonating.

- Similarly, if you are standing with a curved back and too stiff you will not be able to project your voice properly.

- Relax your body and stand in a natural position. This will help you not only project your voice but maintain it for a longer time too.

How important is the volume of my voice?
The volume of your voice depends on the size of your audience. Although you should train yourself to project your voice regardless of the volume, in front of an audience, you vary the volume to support your voice projection.

My voices trembles when I'm nervous and when I try to project it the problem is magnified. What can I do to overcome this obstacle?
This happens because your nervous energy is channelled through your voice. Use your hands and body to channel that energy. Take a deep breath before you start talking. This can help you relax.

Applying the techniques
Now that you know how to articulate the various speech organs and how to project your voice, it is time to put these techniques into action. Read a passage from this book as if you were lecturing on presentation skills. Put some enthusiasm into what you are reading and record your voice using a good quality tape recorder.

As you read, pay particular attention to each letter you pronounce and make a conscious effort to say it the right way. Relax your muscles and let your body cavities resonate as much as possible. Listen to yourself and pay attention to these particular points. Remember that a tape recorder does not reproduce your natural voice and you may sound a bit strange. Do not let this put you off, thinking that your voice does not sound nice.

TRAINING AND LOOKING AFTER YOUR VOICE

All the different aspects of the voice discussed in this chapter so far play an equally important role in the quality of the voice. As with the other muscles of the body, speech muscles need training. Training can take different shapes and forms.

To change your speech habits, which you have developed over several years, is not a simple matter. You need to consciously change them at first, before the change becomes second nature to you. Below are a series of exercises for the different aspects of your voice. Throughout these exercises, use a tape recorder and listen to yourself later and try to improve any deficiencies.

Exercises

Exercise 1

Throw an imaginary ball of out of the window. Say 'haa' and let the pitch of your voice go up the further the ball goes away from you. Imagine that it bounces back towards you and let the pitch of your voice go down, the closer the ball is. Repeat the same exercise saying 'hoo' then 'hay' then 'hee'.

This will exercise your vocal chords as well as your ability to change your pitch. Keep the volume of your voice constant throughout the exercise.

Exercise 2

Try producing the same sound now, imagining an audience in front of you. First address an audience of five people, then project your voice for an audience of fifteen people. Finally imagine an audience of 100 people and try to project your voice accordingly, keeping a constant volume throughout the exercise.

Exercise 3

Read a passage from a story that you like and place the right emphasis and pause to breathe at the right places (commas, full stops, etc.). Think consciously about your breathing and don't hesitate to pause when necessary. This exercise will help control your pauses and breathing.

Exercise 4

Always try to sing no matter how bad you think your voice is or if you can't get the exact tune. Remember you don't have to sing in front of people and certainly you don't need to record your voice in this case.

Looking after your voice

You should always look after your voice in order to maintain it. Below are a few tips on how to avoid losing your voice when you need it.

- Avoid smoking or rooms full of smoke. Giving a presentation after a few drinks in the pub is not a good idea.

- Allow your voice to rest. Even when you are giving a long talk, you can still rest your voice by regular breathing and proper articulation.

- Avoid warm and dry rooms because you risk having a dry throat.

- Don't eat dairy products before your presentation, because the production of mucus is increased and the voice gets rough.

- If you feel that you have a dry mouth and throat, bite your tongue gently. This will produce enough saliva to wet your mouth. Don't bite too hard as you might hurt yourself.

- After a long talk, practise a few relaxing exercises to prepare your voice for rest. These exercises can be stretching, breathing, articulation, etc.

- Avoid cold drinks the night before your speech.

What do I do if I lose my voice in the middle of a presentation?
Pause, have a sip of water. If this doesn't work, give your audience something to do, or think about, while you take a break to relax your voice.

REHEARSING

During your rehearsals, take the voice aspects into consideration all the time. Use the techniques above to develop the right voice for each of your presentations. In order to do that, you need to think about the following factors:

1. the size of your audience

2. the size and acoustics of the room

3. the nature of your talk

4. the period you will be talking for.

Always remember that in a room filled with people, you need to put more energy into projecting your voice than in an empty room.

Following a rehearsal routine
When rehearsing your presentation, you need to follow a certain routine in order to get the right voice. When you work out the emphasis, stress, articulation and projection, you can keep rehearsing until they all come out naturally as part of your script.

For that, you can follow the routine described below:

- Research the size of your audience and the room.
- Determine your projection power.
- Work out your emphasis, stresses and pauses.
- Rehearse.
- Repeat any steps if you feel there is something lacking in your preparations and try to improve on them.

CHECKLIST

1. Using the right voice helps you deliver the right message.

2. Understanding how your voice is produced will help you to improve the tone, pitch, volume and clarity of your speech.

3. An interesting voice will capture the audience's attention.

4. Practise finding the natural pitch of your voice, and then try the various exercises to introduce variations.

5. Effective use of silence and pauses, stress and emphasis will improve the impact of your presentation.

6. Learn to project your voice appropriately.

7. Train your voice using the exercises suggested.

8. Look after your voice – it is a most valuable tool.

CASE STUDIES

Edward sells his technology

Edward is an engineer by training. Through several career development moves, he became a technical salesman. He now has the task of selling hardware for the telecommunications industry. Edward, being an engineer, gets very enthusiastic about technical details and all the fancy things that a piece of equipment can do. He ends up speaking very quickly, with hardly any pauses. Edward is now walking into his manager's room to review his position as a technical salesman.

Sarah uses her voice to succeed

Sarah is a medical doctor. She works in a teaching hospital and her job involves lecturing medical graduates. She is also a member of the local choir. Her musical background makes her appreciate the power of the voice and what effect it can have on people. It also enables her to control it and use it effectively. Having a calm nature, she also pauses often, giving time to the listener to absorb what she has just said.

Her students always look forward to her lectures because, unlike other lecturers, she manages to keep them hooked to the matter in discussion, without getting bored or even feel uncomfortable. Sarah is also successful with her patients. They all love seeing her in the morning, simply because her voice has a calming effect on them.

Lloyd goes to battle

Lloyd is an officer in the army. He regularly gives mission debriefings, usually with a large map in the background as a visual aid. He is used to addressing large groups of soldiers on training missions. He has a very strong voice which projects through the walls of the meeting room.

He is now involved in a real war and has the opportunity of addressing a small group of journalists in a small press conference on the front line. Lloyd uses the same techique, which is a loud voice and no pitch change. The media do not approve of the operations that are going to take place. With Lloyd talking in this way, it does not take them long before they start criticising him.

POINTS TO CONSIDER

1. How could Sarah use her musical talent to make her voice more effective on her listeners?

2. Is changing only the pitch of the voice good enough for capturing the audience's attention?

3. What could Edward do to make his selling more successful?

4. How would a relaxation exercise before a presentation affect your vocal performance?

5. What part does your voice play in making your presentation more successful?

7

Managing Your Audience

SPEAKING YOUR AUDIENCE'S LANGUAGE

Can you speak with a language that is understood by the audience? This is a question you should ask yourself before every presentation. If you can't, then work on it. If you know the language of the country you are presenting in, it is an advantage, but this is not what I mean by 'the audience's language'. What I really mean is the use of words that are easy for the audience to understand.

If your audience prefer pictures and simple language, give them exactly that. Some audiences, usually in conferences, are familiar with technical words, so pitch your presentation at their level of understanding otherwise they may think you are insulting their intelligence.

Different types of audiences

In order to pitch your presentation at the right level and find out what language to speak with, you need to identify the type of audience you are addressing. A few types of audience and the right way to address them are discussed below:

> Recall five different types of audiences you have encountered and what kind of language you used. Which presentation was the most successful?

- Use technical expressions with an *audience of experts*. You do not need to go back to square one and explain the basics as you might be insulting their intelligence as well as boring them by telling them something they already know.

- When addressing an *audience of different ages and backgrounds*, include explanations for those less knowledgeable in the subject without boring the others or insulting their intelligence. Introduce these ideas with a brief explanation like: 'some of you may be familiar with this new scheme, but it is worth explaining it briefly at this stage.'

- On some occasions, the majority of the audience members are *non-experts and of different ages and interests*. This may be the case in a public lecture taking place in a special event. In such a case, assume that your audience's knowledge in the subject is very limited and use the simplest terms and explanations you can. People in the audience who know about the subject will not feel alienated because they understand why you are doing this.

- *Regulate the speed of your presentation to the capacity of the audience to absorb its contents.* Change your speed depending on what you are saying and the importance of the point you are making. When dealing with complicated ideas and important arguments, make sure you go slowly and speak clearly to give your audience time to understand what you are saying.

- *If you notice your audience is becoming impatient*, it may be because you are spending too much time explaining an obvious idea. Try to speed up a little and if necessary cut a few ideas out. If on the other hand you notice that people are getting bored or giving you nervous signs, you might be going too fast for them to keep track of what you are saying. Slow down and take your time in explaining the points that appear to be interesting to the audience.

Always keep in mind the people in the audience you are presenting to. It is their language that you want to speak. Sometimes, you only want to influence five people out of an audience of fifty because it is those five who are going to make a decision after your presentation while the rest are spectators.

Understanding the cultural language

The cultural language of the audience is extremely important. This is especially applicable to presenting abroad or to audiences with different cultural backgrounds. Some jokes may not be understood or may even be offensive. Some people like to be addressed with certain titles and may be offended if addressed otherwise.

You would also take that into consideration when preparing your visual aids. Some pictures may mean different things to your audience. The use of colour is also important. Some people use different colours to indicate different things.

> Write down five cultural habits and customs you know about people of nationalities different from yours.

Your body language is also important in this case. In some countries nodding your head means refusal or rejection. Try to find out about these things before you finalise your preparation. If you travel a lot, it will be easier for you to learn about habits and customs in different countries and cultures.

If you have an audience of mixed cultures, which is usually the case in international conferences, stay on the safe side, avoid making controversial statements and try to use formal language. Use the body language that you feel most comfortable with which will be the most natural one. Follow the general rules described in the previous chapters and don't worry too much about diversions from the usual because these techniques work with people in general, regardless of their culture.

INFLUENCING THEM BY KNOWING THEIR NEEDS

Before you try to convince your audience of a certain idea, it is useful to know what they want out of your presentation and how your proposed idea caters for their needs. Try to find out as much as you can about the people you are presenting to before embarking on the process of preparing for your presentation. The more you know about your audience the easier it is for you to persuade them with your ideas. Presenting is a selling process whether you are expecting members of the audience to buy your product, accept your ideas or even simply agree with you. To make a successful sale, you have to identify your customers as well as their needs.

Selling solutions

Problems exist everywhere. Whether they are personal or general, they can be found in every organisation. These problems can even be global and affect the lives of millions of people. By offering a solution to these problems, your presentation will be a very effective means of communication helping towards selling your ideas.

Here are some ideas for you to consider when trying to convince an audience or sell them something:

- Try to identify the problem or requirements first.

- Arouse the audience's desire by hitting the right chords. There is no point in saying that your new paint formula is odourless to customers who are only interested in its power to resist water.

- Desire may not be directly related to need. If your customers don't really need the product, you can identify their desires and target them. Sometimes people take decisions with their emotions rather than logic. Your product may not be an absolute necessity to the customer, but because it is related to something important emotionally to them they will buy it. A certain manufacturer may need a new machine to add to the production line but desires the latest computer products for his office. This is particularly useful for salesmen, but as far as presentation techniques are concerned, this is another factor to keep in mind when presenting an idea or product.

- Try to find out about their personal thoughts from decisions they made in the past – who they are and what they have done. If you expect to be presenting to someone who worked as a junior researcher for a motor manufacturer and now is a manger with an electronics company, try to use their knowledge in the motor industry to illustrate a point and arouse their nostalgic feelings. Refer to golf if you know there is a golfer in the room. This might help arouse his or her interest in the product simply by relating it to an area of their personal interest.

READING YOUR AUDIENCE

Sometimes you can find out about people as you are presenting. You can tell whether they are convinced or pleased from their body language. You can change your pace or stresses on certain points according to the feedback you get from the audience. There are several things you can notice about people in the audience which tell you how they are reacting to your talk. To notice this, however, you should keep eye contact with the key persons in the room. Here are some of the most common signs given by audiences and their meanings:

Spotting signs of interest and lack of it
Posture
Observe the angle at which the body is positioned. If the person is

leaning forward he is showing an interest and a desire to be involved in your talk. You are most likely to receive the first question from this category of people. Sometimes people get tired from this position and choose to sit back. This may not necessarily mean they have lost interest.

Arms and legs
To find out whether they are still interested, check some other signs. If their legs or arms are crossed, or they have their hand over their mouths, they are forming barriers between you and them which shows their lack of interest.

Eyes
Another sign is the position of their eyes. If they are looking at the visual aid or keeping direct eye contact with you it means they are still interested. If, however, their eyes are wandering around the room, or they are looking out of the window, you should do something about it quickly and try to seize their attention again. A sudden change in the pitch of your voice might be appropriate.

Coughing
Sometimes people start coughing, or clearing their throat, when they lose interest in the talk, as opposed to holding their breath when they are highly interested. This can be distracting to other members of the audience who are trying to concentrate. It can also be contagious sometimes, because some people feel embarrassed to clear their throats and wait for someone else to start it so it becomes a group activity. Don't let this put you off. Change the speed of your talk and skip to more interesting ideas.

Nodding
The most reassuring sign is when someone in the audience is nodding his or her head. By doing this, they clearly want to show you their agreement with what you are telling them and encourage you to tell them more. Look at those people every time you feel nervous or unsure about your feelings.

Spotting signs of discontent and unease
The presentation is a one-sided conversation until you start taking questions. Deal with the situation as a normal conversation, thinking of the audience as the other person. The only difference is that you have several people to talk to and the only feedback you

get from them is their body language.

In a normal conversation, when the person opposite you starts to place barriers between you both by crossing legs or holding their hands in front of them to protect the front part of their body, they are giving defensive signs because they may feel threatened by your ideas or strongly disagree with you. Maybe you have hit a sensitive point which makes them feel defensive. The same can apply to your audience. Try not to respond by being defensive yourself. Keep an inviting tone and body language to avoid any escalation in the display of unease.

In the list below, give a mark from 1 to 10 for each of the states you usually put your audience in. Next to each one below 6, write a suggestion on how you could do better.

State	Mark	Improvement
Interest	....	....
Unthreatened	....	....
Agreement with you	....	....
Nods	....	....
Eye contact with you or the visual aid	....	....

AVOIDING CONFLICT – 'LOVE THY AUDIENCE'

It is very common for presenters to be thought of as potential liars. You often hear remarks from the audience such as 'I'm not sure about these figures' or 'are you sure this is the best way to deal with this problem?' The hostile environment which exists between presenters and audiences is not produced by the audience only. Presenters are also responsible for the tension that exists in some audience-presenter relations.

If you walk into the room thinking that your audience are the enemy and that you are going to defeat them by convincing them of your ideas, you are very likely to encounter some fierce opposition.

Handling escalation of conflicts

Sometimes, presenters tend to react aggressively to actions taken or words said by members of the audience. This aggressive reaction is often responded to by an even sharper response, resulting in an escalation of the problem. To prevent this kind of tension, you, as the presenter, should:

- think of your audience as friends even though you know what they are thinking about you

- take the first step in starting a friendly relationship with them

- avoid attacking them directly and losing your nerve, simply because you think someone out there is trying to get you.

When you are friendly to them, you can intimidate the biggest bully without taking any action that justifies his suspicions. Be respectful all the time and keep a smile on your face when confronted with aggression. This will help the offensive person to back off. If you react in a defensive way, you give them further reason for being offensive.

Disagreeing with your audience

You should respect your audience so they respect you. Don't be afraid of disagreeing with an idea, or saying no to a proposition. You are entitled to your own opinion and you have the right to explain yourself. The nasty man in the audience said to the presenter: 'Are you expecting us to pay all that money for developing your proposed system?' The presenter replied with a smile: 'Yes, (pause) I'm sure five million account units are negligible when you consider the return on investment.'

By saying 'yes' and then pausing, you create an element of shock. This might result in a laugh from the audience, or a great silence. You then give your justification. The person who asked the question will not be encouraged to carry on with the same line of questioning and may even be impressed by the way you frankly answered the question.

How would you react to each of the following situations?

1. Someone asking sarcastic and negative questions.

2. Someone talking to you aggressively with a loud voice.

3. Someone frowning at you every time you suggest something.

Earning respect
Earning respect is another reward for being friendly to your audience. By respecting them and their opinion, they have no reason to disrespect you and not treat you seriously.

Avoiding arrogance
Sometimes, your audience have a higher position than yourself, or are experts in the field of your expertise. In this situation:

- Don't be put off by the fact that they might know more about the subject than you do.

- Make sure you show them your knowledge and impress them with your confidence in what you are saying.

- Don't go to the extent of showing off and being arrogant because then I am sure they will do their best to 'break your neck'.

Admitting your mistakes
It is very easy for people to spot your mistakes, especially when they know a great deal about the subject or object you are presenting. The easiest way to lose respect is to make a mistake and then try to ignore it. If you do 99 per cent of your work properly, one mistake may ruin everything.

As they say, 'to err is human'. For as long as we live, we are very likely to make mistakes especially when under pressure. These mistakes, however, can be turned to advantage. How? Easy – simply admit them.

The audience is more likely to forgive you if you admit you made a certain mistake rather than trying to bluff your way out of it or blame someone else. Don't, however, be very apologetic and go over the top by begging for mercy.

Handling apologies

A member of the audience suggests that your estimated cost of the project is wrong. You check the number on the slide and find out it is not what you originally had in your report. What do you think the best answer would be?

(a) 'I'm sorry, it is my fault, this figure should be $300k and not $30k. I hope it didn't cause any misunderstanding.'

(b) 'This is an approximate figure and may vary according to the salaries and number of employees working on the project.'

(c) 'I'm terribly sorry, I didn't mean to write this number on the slide. It must have been the secretary who typed it. I apologise if it caused any misunderstanding.'

Answer (a) contains an apology and admission of guilt. This is very likely to gain you forgiveness. It will also earn you respect for the courage and politeness that exist in your answer. If Mr Nasty in the audience doesn't want to forgive you, at least you will have given him a chance.

Everybody now knows that the figure is wrong and the size of the error is big. There is no point in trying to justify it by giving answer (b). By giving this answer, you will lose your respect and the audience won't take you seriously.

The worse answer to give is (c). It is over-apologetic and puts the blame on someone else. Compare it with (a). The use of 'I hope' is much better than another apology which makes you look weak and insecure. Taking the blame or at least not blaming someone else, earns you more respect.

INVOLVING YOUR AUDIENCE

I have already emphasised that keeping the audience interested in your talk is a very important aspect of your presentation. If your presentation is an interactive process, in which you and the audience can contribute to the events taking place in the room, you will certainly convince them of your idea and get the message across in a very short time.

There are several ways in which the audience can participate. Whether on an individual basis or in groups they can be involved in proving certain points or contributing to the contents of the presentation.

Letting your audience participate in demonstrations helps to keep them interested in your talk and makes them feel active in the process of explanation. If they do things by themselves they are more likely to remember the idea behind the demonstration.

Asking questions

Asking for a show of hands makes them think about your question and actively find out what they think about it. Not all of them may decide to participate, but they surely will think about what you said rather than listen to it passively. For example, the question 'How many of you have participated in similar projects?' can be followed by 'I'm sure, then, that most of you will realise how large the amount of work involved is.' The question gave them the chance to think about the project, some of them answered and were proud to make their participation in the project known, and surely most of them will remember that there is a great deal of work involved in the project.

Asking for a show of hands is not appropriate on all occasions. You should do this only when you feel that the audience are receptive to the idea. If you are presenting to a small audience where you more or less know the expertise and experience of most of the members, you don't need to ask such questions.

Using questionnaires

With larger audiences, especially in large lectures and product launch presentations, audience involvement is very important and can influence the outcome of the presentation. There you can involve the audience in less formal ways. A show of hands can be more common than in highly formal situations. You can hand out short questionnaires and get someone to collect them and give the results. Plan this very carefully in a way not to interfere with the flow of your presentation. Handling questionnaires can be a very delicate matter. Here are some tips that may help you in dealing with this type of audience involvement:

- Don't put too many questions on the questionnaire.

- Make it short and phrase your questions in a way that you can more or less guess the answers.

- Get the help of someone else to collect the papers, giving the audience a short break.

- You can, instead of handing out questionnaires, make use of electronic polling systems and get the results straight onto a computer screen.

- Only use questionnaires when you feel they are necessary in order to prove a point. Things can go wrong and you may get the opposite effect.

Using demonstrations

The most entertaining way to involve the audience is getting volunteers to participate in live demonstrations or to help the presenter to illustrate some ideas. Here are some guidelines:

- Choose a volunteer who you feel would fit the role to be performed. A tall person could represent an antenna, for example.

- Look out for those who look uninterested in your talk and choose them to perform a simple demonstration. This will give them a certain element of excitement and make them more interested in the presentation later.

- Keep your demonstrations simple. You don't want to confuse a volunteer on stage and embarrass him or her.

- All your demonstrations should be basic and well within the capabilities of your volunteers to conduct them. Don't for instance, ask people to run a computer program they've never seen before.

- A demonstration doesn't have to be purely scientific and serious – it can involve an element of humour. This helps the audience remember that particular moment for quite a long time because they associated it with a funny or terrible joke, whichever way they felt about it.

Using volunteers

Handling volunteers can be difficult sometimes. They are very likely to be nervous and might do some strange things to channel their nervous energy. Be very friendly with them and try not to push them around as happens on some television shows, where the host's assistant brings the contestants to their spots and pushes them around to face the camera, as quickly as possible. This action can be concealed by the camera but not from the live audience.

When working with volunteers, try to remember the following few simple rules:

1. Be patient with your volunteers.

2. Start by asking them their names and where they come from to help them relax and get used to being in the spotlight.

3. Call them by their names – this creates a friendly environment and helps them relax too.

4. Try to keep some distance from your volunteers. Some people surround themselves with an imaginary barrier marking their personal territory, which they don't like to be invaded. In television, show hosts tend to stay very close to their contestants, to get in the field of view of the camera. With live audiences this is unnecessary – they can see both of you on stage, wherever you are.

5. Get someone to explain the boring details to your volunteers aside, while you tell your audience the general principles of the demonstration.

6. After they have finished their task, thank the volunteers and provoke the audience to applaud with the tone of your voice. If they don't react in this way, ask them to 'put their hands together for the brave volunteers who did a great job'.

PLANTING QUESTIONS

If you know your audience well enough, you can more or less guess what they might ask you. More importantly, you know how to make them ask you what you want. You know what most of them will be interested in and can plant questions, for them to ask you later.

Statements are usually the main cause of curiosity. 'We were confronted with two choices. To reduce the cost or to make a better quality product. We opted for the latter.' Stopping there without any further explanation is a very dangerous statement which will raise several questions. Those who disagree with you will seize the first opportunity to corner you. At that point you can give a clear and detailed explanation that you prepared earlier.

Guidelines for planting questions

- Try to hit the right chords. If you know that someone in the audience feels strongly about a certain issue, mention it in a positive way. This will encourage them to show their agreement with you and ask you to expand on the idea. When given the chance, you can expand on it in the way you want so long as you prepare yourself for such an explanation.

- Make sure that the points you want to be asked about later are clearly mentioned in your presentation. Go through them slowly and make sure everybody understands what you are saying. Most of the questions come from the people who understand your presentation and want to know more about a certain point and not from those who didn't understand a word.

- Remember that people who understand are more likely to ask relevant questions and fall into the trap you've set them. Those who don't understand your talk tend to ask you irrelevant or sometimes strange questions. The way to deal with those questions is considered later in this chapter.

- Be prepared to answer the questions you are planting. You can be very busy planting them, and forget to prepare the answers.

What do I do if I plant a question but no one picks it up during question time?
If it is an important issue that you want to expand on, you can use an opportunity within another answer to come back to this point. You can also expand on it without being asked to do so.

Using 'accomplices'

Some people use a different tactic. They ask friends in the audience to ask them certain questions that they prepared earlier. When people start raising their hands to ask questions, the presenter chooses his planted accomplices. This works if no one else knows the relation between the presenter and his or her friends in disguise. Although this might work, it is still called cheating. It's up to you to decide whether you really want to work in this way.

Most importantly, when answering this type of question, don't let it show that you are expecting it. Take a short time to think about it as you would do with the unexpected questions and give your answer with a confident tone. I'm sure you wouldn't even think about reading it out from a pre-written script. Would you?

Planting further questions

Some answers can lead to further questions and if this can happen naturally, you can also make it happen deliberately if you like. You can plant further questions in your answers. The same techniques apply: use the half-justified statement or the decisions made about choices to provoke further inquiries. This, however, can be very difficult and can easily get out of hand. Don't do it if you are not sure about what you are doing.

Telling the audience what they want to know

If your time is limited and you can't say the whole truth, take your time in answering the questions you prepared, but remember it is not only what *you* decide to tell your audience that matters. You need to tell them what they want to know, in order to convince them. There is no point spending all the time answering questions that you feel confident about. They might want to know about something else, which is really interesting to them. Give them the chance to ask you about it.

ANSWERING QUESTIONS

This is a chance for you to expand and build on what you said in your presentation. Whether the questions were planted in your presentation or result from the need of the audience to know more, it is your chance to find out what the audience is thinking about your talk.

Using the feedback

Up to the time of taking questions, the only feedback you have from the audience is their body language. This can tell you a lot about them, but it is not very accurate and can be misleading. When you start dealing with questions, you find out more about individuals in the audience. You know who really is a friend and who's Mr Nasty.

It is very important to know what members of the audience are thinking and by asking questions, they reveal their thoughts to you.

You can know what they really want from your product or proposal. A question about the cost comes from the person who is worried about money. Who do you think a question about safety comes from? Perhaps someone who is worried about insurance premiums.

The situation here is well known to sales people. A good salesperson tries to find out what the customer really wants which makes it possible for them to sell at a higher price. Some sales people try to convince you to buy what they want to sell rather than what you want to buy. If you don't give your audience the chance to tell you what they really want and give you hints as to why they want it, it will be difficult for you to convince them with your proposals. From their questions you can tell what they want and answer them accordingly. Although it is useful for you to answer planted questions, you should also give the audience a chance to ask you what they have in mind.

> Can you recall an occasion when someone tried to sell you something you didn't want? Review three occasions when you bought them and your feelings about it some time after the purchase.

Dealing with questions

Here are a few rules to keep in mind when dealing with questions:

- Make sure you tell the audience that they can ask questions at the end of the presentation. This gives them the chance to think of what they want to ask during your talk.

- Avoid telling them to interrupt you during the presentation. If they do, they may interrupt your train of thought and your presentation may take much longer than anticipated.

- It is always difficult to ask the first question, so break the ice by saying something like: 'I'm often asked...' or 'What did you think about (something you mentioned in your presentation)? Do you agree with that?' This will help jump start them and provide a starting point for you to emphasise what you said earlier.

- When giving your answer, don't only talk to the person who asked the question but to the whole audience. The others will then not feel excluded from the discussion.

- If the question couldn't be heard by the entire audience, make sure everyone knows what the question was by repeating it or putting it in your own words before you answer it.

- Sometimes, people will say something which isn't really a question at all. It can be a statement of their opinion or a reinforcement of something you said or even an attempt to look clever. Thank them for making this point, reinstate your own argument, if necessary, and move on to the next question.

- Don't try to bluff your way through a question you can't answer. Tell them that you can't answer it and you need to check your sources. You can say that you'll come back to them about it. If you have to answer on the spot, it would be useful to have some back-up information handy to refer to. Most presentations are accompanied by reports. If you know that the answer is in the report you can tell the questioner so.

Sometimes I get asked a question that I'm very happy to answer and end up giving a long detailed explanation. Is this a good or a bad thing?
Don't make another presentation out of answering those questions, simply because you know the answers or you've prepared them. Give every topic the necessary time according to importance and influence on the audience and not the amount of knowledge you have on the subject in hand.

When the questioner has misunderstood
Sometimes you get a question from someone who didn't really understand what you said. 'You said that the space probe will run out of power before the end of the mission. Why?' What do you think the right answer could be?

(a) 'You completely misunderstood what I said...'

(b) 'This is not true, you completely missed the point, let me explain...'

(c) 'This isn't what really happens. The probe will accomplish its mission before it runs out of power...'

I'm sure you will agree that the best answer is (c). It doesn't insult the intelligence of the person asking the question, like answer (a). Answer (b) is even more offensive, because it contains two attacks on the person. The first is a direct accusation that what he or she is saying is false and the second is a suggestion that they did not understand what you said.

Handling difficult questions
There are some questions that you don't expect or hope you'd never be asked, for various reasons. When faced with this type of question:

1. Don't panic.

2. Take your time to think about it and don't rush into an answer without assembling your thoughts.

3. Keep it brief and to the point. Sometimes people tend to talk until they are interrupted. It is very unlikely that someone will interrupt you. After all, this is a presentation not an interview.

4. If you feel you are drifting from the main point and trying to find words to expand your answer, it is time to stop with a concluding remark.

Handling Mr Nasty
If someone is playing the bad guy by challenging you and starting a verbal fight:

1. Don't become defensive and let your body language show it.

2. Maintain an open posture and keep your inviting tone.

3. Restate your opinion and put your argument in a different way if possible.

If, after all the attempts to answer his questions, Mr Nasty insists on going ahead with his challenge, what do I do?
Tell him that his dialogue is interesting and that you would be willing to have a private talk with him after the meeting. Then turn your eyes away and ask for the next question.

Using visual aids
Use any extra slides you made, to explain any points brought up by

the audience through questions. Question time is part of the presentation and using visual aids helps you answer the questions and gives the impression that you are enthusiastic and have spent some time preparing extra slides for your presentation.

After the presentation
When your time is up, stop taking questions by thanking your audience for their time and the organisers for giving you the opportunity to address this particular audience. Some people might come to you after the presentation to have a quick chat. Answer them briefly and spend some time with them if you can. Some of the most effective points can be mentioned during this time, so don't underestimate its importance.

CHECKLIST

1. Identify the audience's language.

2. Be aware of cultural differences and customs.

3. Know your audience's needs.

4. Learn to read your audience by observing their body language.

5. Always think of your audience as your friends, not the enemy.

6. Handle aggression by being open and respectful.

7. Be willing to admit your mistakes.

8. Involve your audience by asking questions or using demonstrations.

9. Use your presentation to 'plant' questions in the minds of the audience.

10. Welcome questions as telling you what the audience want to know.

11. Plan how to handle silly or difficult questions.

CASE STUDIES

Jonathan presents a paper

Jonathan is a researcher. He is presenting one of his newly published papers on the effect of car exhausts on the environment of metropolitan areas. This presentation is part of a competition and the audience includes his fellow researchers and a panel of judges to assess him.

He looks at his friends most of the time and when he finds that they are getting bored, he speeds up his talk. When signs of interest arise from some of his friends, he slows down and elaborates on the point in hand.

During his presentation, he criticises the work of one of the judges, without naming her of course. The audience knows who he is talking about and agree with him. He gains their trust and friendship.

The majority of the spectators in the room are impressed with his presentation and think he should win the competition. After all, he is saying the things they want to hear. When the result comes out, everybody is shocked.

Malik presents his project

Malik, a university student, is presenting his final year project to a panel of lecturers. He talks to them as if they were his apprentices in a summer job. He explains to them what they already know, in a patronising tone. Then suddenly, he looks at his watch and says, 'How am I doing? – Oh God!' I have never seen a person panicking like that before. He starts rushing his talk like mad, because he is running out of time.

After he bombards the audience with his fast-moving sentences, and the people in the front row are showered with saliva the presentation comes to an end. He sighs and returns to his lecturing tone to announce, to the relief of the audience and certainly the panel members, that he is ready to take questions.

In an attempt to show that he is relaxed, he leans on an elevated bench behind him. He nearly sleeps on it. His attitude makes the lecturers ask him the most difficult and nasty questions they can come up with. He gets confused by the sheer difficulty of the questions and starts talking nonsense just to save his skin. He doesn't get a good mark, by the way.

Sales people conduct a survey

A group is presenting a new piece of hardware (incorporating a fax machine, phone and personal computer in one) to win a consultancy contract for a large manufacturer. They pass a questionnaire around asking the audience to answer a number of questions about their needs. Although the questions are related to the project, they do not prove any points or even relate to the presentation. They create a big confusion trying to pass them around when everybody is trying to listen to the presentation. The intention appears to be to make people think about their needs.

Most of the audience members feel that their intelligence is being insulted. No one even bothers to collect the questionnaire and announce the results. The outcome is the failure of the group to secure a contract.

POINTS TO CONSIDER

1. What were Jonathan's mistakes and how could he avoid them?

2. In an audience of a mixture of people including spectators and people who can make decisions, who should you be addressing?

3. How could Malik have done better? What were his mistakes?

4. How do you deal with questions that you can't answer?

8

Putting It All Together

SETTING THE ENVIRONMENT

Now that you have the tools and expertise to deliver a good presentation, it is time to put everything together in an excellent performance. No matter what you think of presentations, you should always treat them as a small performance. Performing in front of an audience involves not only you but your surroundings as well. The stage has a great effect on theatrical performances and so does the room in which you are presenting on your presentation.

The visual aids you use play an essential role towards the success of your presentation and their use should be planned as the use of lighting is planned for a play.

Choosing the right place

There are several types of place where you may find yourself giving a presentation. These can vary from a small, over-ventilated room to a large, warm lecture theatre. You may not find the perfect environment, but you should always try to look for the nearest to perfect.

For a good setting, a room should have the following characteristics:

1. Large enough to fit all the people invited or expected to attend.

2. Temperature control is working properly and the ambient temperature is moderate and not too warm.

3. All the seats are positioned in such a way that no one has to break his/her neck in order to see you or your visual aids.

4. Enough space is provided for visual aids (flip chart, OHP, etc.).

5. The lighting is controllable or at the right level for your slides to be seen. If the room has too many windows and you are

presenting on a sunny day, make sure that there are curtains to close, otherwise your projected slides may appear very faint.

6. The room has enough power points located close to the electrical equipment you want to use.

7. The acoustics are suitable for the presentation. Too much echo is not what you want. In larger rooms, the use of a sound amplification system might be needed.

If you have a chance to go into the room some time before the presentation, look out for aspects that you can improve to fit the above criteria. For instance, if the ventilation is not suitable, try changing the temperature settings if the controls are in the room or ask whoever is responsible for it to change it for you.

From your past experience with presentations, think of three more things you can change in a room to fit the criteria listed above.

I sometimes don't know the size of the audience. How can I then find the right room?
If there is no way you can tell the approximate size of the audience, go for a large room to be on the safe side. If your audience turns out to be much smaller than you expected, ask them to occupy the seats nearer to you.

Customising the environment
Take a good look at the room. Check the following environmental effects and try to act accordingly:

*   If you notice that there is a clock on the wall which can be seen by the audience, try to hide it (with a flip chart, for example) or remove it altogether. This is because people tend to look at the time and feel that it is not passing quickly enough.

*   Close any windows that overlook a busy street, to avoid noise pollution in the room. If the room is too warm and you feel the need to open a window, do so before the presentation and close it just before you start.

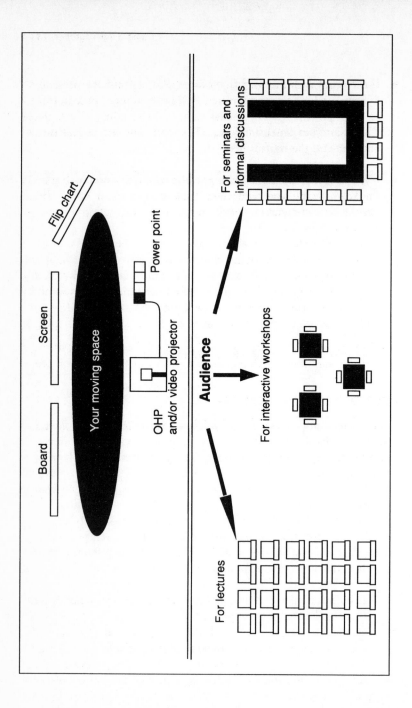

Fig. 9. Various room layouts.

- If the room is small, with an elevated platform for the presenter to stand on, arrange the seating to give you enough space in front of the platform. Use this space and avoid standing at a higher level than your small audience. This can only intimidate them and increase the barrier between you.

- If you can rearrange the seating in the room, always try to place the seats facing you with their back to the room door. This enables late-comers to sneak in without distracting people's attention from you.

- In large lecture theatres, make sure that the lighting is controlled, so when you start your presentation it is dimmed in the audience section. This helps the audience focus on you and your visual aids. However, it shouldn't be too dark for the audience to take notes if they want to.

See Figure 9 for some examples of room layouts.

PRESENTING WITH A GROUP

Group presentations are not uncommon. Sometimes you may find yourself having to present with one or more people. This is very common among university students or teams at the end of group projects or competitions.

Performing together

In this case it pays off if the whole group rehearse thoroughly and co-ordinate in order to keep the flow of ideas without many interruptions between the sections presented by different team members. When presenting with a group, remember that:

- This is a group performance and co-ordination plays an essential role in the success of your presentation.

- If you feel that you haven't had enough time to rehearse together and co-ordinate your actions and talks, use prompts as a reminder for individuals to start their part of the presentation.

- The group should be introduced at the beginning of the presentation, first as a group, then each individual should be presented in turn. This gives the audience an idea of who's who if they aren't familiar with the faces of your team members.

- Try to make the introduction as brief as possible without too many details, otherwise you risk boring the audience before you start the presentation.

- The presentation should be divided so that the change from one member to another follows a logical change in the contents of the presentation and acts as a short pause for the audience to absorb the ideas.

- The change-over should be smooth and hardly noticed by the audience. The prompt could be, for instance, a question where the answer is provided by the next speaker. Another way is simply to introduce the next topic together with the person presenting it, e.g. 'So how was the project implemented within the given time and resources? Fred will tell us about project management.'

- Always keep in mind that you will win as a team and there is no reason why one individual should gain more credit than another. The presentation should be worded in such a way that the whole team gets the credit and not the individual presenting a certain achievement.

- Support and respect are of paramount importance in group presentations. If you feel that a team member is in need of help, don't hesitate to intervene.

Showing respect

In order to be taken seriously, you need to show respect towards your colleagues as well as your audience. Here are a few hints on how to do that:

- When taking questions, don't try to answer them on your own, share them with the group. If you find that one of your colleagues can give a better answer or stands a better chance of convincing the audience, let them answer the question.

- Show your respect by suggesting that your colleague is an expert in this area and can give a more precise answer. This also makes the person asking the question believe they are a bit special to have this person answer their question.

- Personal jealousy may sometimes prevent you from saying good things about a colleague and making him/her look better than you, but if you overcome that obstacle, you have a powerful tool that can tip the balance in favour of your team.

- Don't try to score individual points at the expense of the group. Remember, there are no points to be scored individually. You may not agree with a certain group decision in which case you can let a colleague defend the point.

- After the presentation, discuss the team performance with your colleagues and try to assess what went well and what can be improved in the future.

- Avoid tension between team members as this may be reflected in your presentations and makes it harder for you to apply the techniques discussed above.

- Always remember that you want the success of the entire group and not individuals.

COPING WITH STAGE FRIGHT

Stage fright is suffered by most, if not all, people in the spotlight, including actors, television show hosts, public speakers and even politicians. It may not be apparent to us when we watch them, but they have all experienced stage fright at one point or another.

The very thought of speaking in public may frighten some people. When the nervousness and the rush of adrenalin get out of control, the effects can be disastrous, but if controlled, they can improve a presenter's performance.

Recognising the symptoms
The symptoms of stage fright can be apparent in several ways:

(a) your neck and shoulders may feel stiff
(b) your mouth may be dry or the extreme opposite
(c) you may even feel physically sick
(d) your heart pumps faster and, to you, louder.

No matter how frightening the symptoms themselves are, remember that they can be helpful. Many well-known public speakers and actors use their nervousness to give memorable performances. They are able to channel all the nervous energy into their performance which help lift it up.

It is very rewarding when you deliver a good presentation and you get a positive response from the audience. This repays for all the suffering you had at the beginning when you were frightened. Keep that in your mind when the dreaded symptoms start to appear.

There are two types of cure for stage fright: mental and physical.

Mental cures for stage fright

You need to have the right frame of mind in order to overcome the effects of stage fright. Here are some points to remember which can help you control your nervousness:

- Prepare well for your presentation and rehearse enough times to become confident. You should also be comfortable with all the ideas you are presenting as this is one major contributor to your fright before a presentation.

- Spend a few moments before the presentation visualising it in your mind, by reviewing its structure and the main points and messages it includes.

- If you are not reading from a script or note cards, have a written summary of the main points ready and at a short distance from you to use if needed. I always have one but have never needed it so far, although the thought of having it there has helped boost my confidence.

- No matter how nervous you feel with all the symptoms that you are experiencing, many of these symptoms will be apparent to you only. The audience only notice the apparent physical symptoms and in many cases they don't even pay attention to them, unless they are greatly affecting your presentation.

- Remember that the audience share your fear of public speaking and they are on your side. Even those who want to disagree with you, still want to be stimulated and challenged by the contents of your presentation.

- If you don't get a reaction from the audience this may be due to them being taken by what you are saying. You will be surprised at the number of people who absorb most of what you say without nodding their heads, even once, during your presentation.

- It will also help if you have something nice to look forward to after the presentation, to relax and avoid an anti-climax after a good performance.

- Always consider what went well in your presentation and what can be improved for the next time. In many cases you will find that more preparation would have made you more confident.

Physical cures for stage fright
The physical aspects of stage fright may be dealt with by doing the following:

- Relax your muscles. Go from your neck to your feet warming up each muscle in turn. Give yourself some time to relax before the presentation. Warm muscles can cope better with tension.

- Run through some of your speech, exercising your vocal chords by changing the volume and pitch. Exercise your facial muscles by exaggerating your facial expressions, as you go through part of your talk.

- Take a deep breath from the level of your stomach and breathe out slowly. Repeat that a few times.

- Release the tension in your neck by nodding and lifting your head several times. Don't stand with your knees and ankles tense because they will tend to shiver.

Above all, try to channel the nervous energy into your presentation to make you sound more energetic and enthusiastic. Remember that most of the symptoms are only apparent to you and all you need is to try and hide the rest from the audience, by reducing the level of nervousness you have.

I feel extremely nervous every time I give a presentation. People keep reassuring me that my presentations are good, but how do I know that they are telling the truth?

They might very well be telling the truth. Remember that the stage fright symptoms are more apparent to you than to the audience. You know that you are extremely nervous, but all they know is what they see. Use a video camera to tape yourself. You will most likely find out that your nervousness hardly shows on the outside. If there are any apparent nervous signs that you can spot on the film try to avoid them the next time.

PRODUCING A PRESENTATION CHECKLIST

Like a pilot before a flight, you need to have a checklist to remind you of what you have to do before your presentation. There are two different types of checklist:

1. For a day or two prior to the presentation day, to be used in the preparations for the final day.

2. For the day on which the presentation is taking place, to be used a few hours before the presentation starts.

Some of the items are present on both checklists, to double check that nothing is missing from the essential ingredients.

Preliminary checklists

The checklist which should be used a day or two before the presentation should include the following:

● Slides are ready and printed on transparencies.

● Any equipment that needs to be ordered beforehand is already ordered.

● Rehearsals should be finalised if not yet completed.

● If using a video, it should be forwarded to the required position.

● A final estimate of the number of attendees.

● For live demonstrations: demonstration tried and rehearsed. All required materials available.

- All the necessary arrangements made for the room or hall to be used.

- You know where the venue is and you know how long it takes you to get there.

- Any support notes are printed and made ready for handing out.

> Identify five more things you need to remember a few days before your presentation.

On the day of your presentation, try to arrive at least one hour before the start, to have enough time to go through your checklist. Some of the items on the list may not apply to your case, so do not worry about them. If you cannot tick some of the items off, estimate their effect on your presentation – if it is not too critical, skip them.

Checklist for the day itself
The checklist for the day should include the following:

- You are well dressed for the occasion.

- All the slides are complete and in order.

- All the equipment that you need is in the room and properly set up.

- Any electrical appliances that you are using are operational.

- Power points positioned conveniently close to the equipment.

- If you are using a flip chart, check if it has enough pages for you to use.

- If you are using a board, make sure you have the appropriate writing materials.

- Suitable pointer for every visual aid is available.

- If reading from cards, make sure that they are in order.

- For live demonstrations make sure that what you need is available and ready to be used quickly.

- Make sure that you have the means of telling the time (clock at the back of the room, watch, etc.).

- A glass of water is available next to you in case you need it.

- If you need members of the audience to help you in demonstrations, you might want to talk to them beforehand.

- Supporting notes and handouts are with you.

- No barriers are present between you and the audience.

- If applicable, the sound system is operational and at the right level.

- Any lighting arrangements are agreed with the lighting person assisting on the day.

Can you think of any other things you need to remember on the day? Draw up a list of five of these.

SURVIVING UNEXPECTED PROBLEMS

You may find yourself in a situation where, in the middle of your presentation, something does not go according to your plan. In order to deal with this kind of situation, do the following:

- Always be prepared for the worst.

- Think of an alternative plan, to use in emergencies.

- Be prepared to give your presentation without visual aids, because the equipment may break down in the middle of the presentation.

- Prepare alternative visual aids. This is particularly important if you are using a computer view panel. These tend to heat up and play all sorts of tricks. You can always revert to a less sophisticated technology, like printed slides, if the panel breaks down.

Write a contingency plan for each of the following situations:

1. OHP breaks down

2. Slide projector does not work

3. Flip chart runs out of paper

4. OHP breaks down, no secondary bulb

5. Room gets too warm

6. No board in the room

CHECKLIST

1. Check out the room where you will give your presentation. Pay attention to size, temperature, seating, lighting, power points and acoustics.

2. If you can, rearrange the room to make it more suitable for you.

3. Group presentations must be well rehearsed and co-ordinated.

4. It is important for all members of the group to respect the others and to work as a team.

5. Stage fright can be handled by adopting the right mental approach and by learning relaxation techniques.

6. Draw up two checklists: one for your preparations and one for the presentation day itself.

7. Draw up contingency plans for any problems that may arise.

8. Be prepared for the unexpected!

CASE STUDIES

Getting group support

Two groups of surgeons are presenting new organ transplant procedures at a medical conference. In the first group, the person speaking needs to point at the large diagram behind him to show the incision point. He realises that he doesn't have his pointer. He starts stretching and jumping to point at the correct section of the diagram. None of his colleagues moves a muscle to do anything.

In the following group, the presenter realises that the pointer is missing. One of his colleagues stands up naturally and offers him her pointer without any sign of panic. The presentation goes on smoothly.

Margaret forgets her checklist

Margaret is a policewoman. She is attending a local neighbourhood watch meeting and is asked to give a presentation advising the local residents on actions to take in order to prevent crime.

She needs to show her audience a list of actions to take, as well as some simple diagrams to illustrate her points. Being a busy officer, she did not have time before the presentation to go through her checklist and assumed that everything was going to be fine.

In the middle of her presentation, the OHP breaks down. She quickly switches to the secondary bulb which doesn't work either.

Margaret keeps calm. Instead of the OHP, she uses the flip chart that she had asked for on the day before the presentation.

Graham arranges the room

Graham is a property surveyor. He is asked to give a presentation to a group of people who work for the local council on the state of council property in the area. He sends a general invitation to their manager giving him the date and the venue details.

He books a room in his building from the facilities department, specifically for that presentation. On the day, twice as many people as the room can accommodate turn up, so most of them don't get seats and have to stand up. The ventilation system can't cope with the heat generated by that many people, so Graham opens the window to let some fresh air in. The window lets in not only fresh air, but also all the noise from a busy street below. The audience don't learn much about the state of the council buildings.

POINTS TO CONSIDER

1. What are the good and bad decisions that Margaret made?

2. How important is it to create the right environment for a presentation and why?

3. What could Graham have done to avoid the problem he had?

4. How can you use stage fright to your advantage?

9

Learning and Developing

ASSESSING THE RESULTS

At the end of each presentation, you are most likely to find yourself thinking about it, even if you don't intend to. It is always useful to reflect back on your performance during each presentation, to try to identify the aspects that went well and, of course, what went wrong.

Your presentation could be a success or a failure in the eyes of your audience, but in your eyes, the results may be different. In order to find out whether you've done well or not you need to assess the results. There are several ways of doing this:

- Observe the feedback from your audience afterwards. This tells you a lot about whether they enjoyed your talk or not.

- Look at the quantity and the quality of enquiries you receive after the presentation. If people ask meaningful questions, the chances are they enjoyed your presentation and understood your ideas.

- If it is a sales presentation, the obvious positive result will be securing a sale. However, on many occasions, you may deliver a good presentation but not a winning one. This may be because your product is not what the customer is looking for. This is not necessarily a failure on your part.

- If you have friends in the audience, ask them for their honest opinion afterwards. They are the ones who can tell you how you performed from the audience's point of view.

- If you have the facility to record your presentation on video tape, do so and watch it later. This gives you the most honest opinion of all. A camera does not lie, it tells you the truth, the whole truth and nothing but the truth.

Rate yourself

In the following table, rate the different aspects of a presentation you have delivered before reading this book. Use the same table to assess yourself after presentations to be delivered in the future:

1. Visual aids	1	2	3	4	5
2. Structure	1	2	3	4	5
3. Body language	1	2	3	4	5
4. Audience reaction	1	2	3	4	5
5. Voice projection	1	2	3	4	5
6. Dealing with stage fright	1	2	3	4	5
7. Dealing with questions	1	2	3	4	5

An average score of three or more indicates a good performance. Try to do this assessment looking at yourself on a video tape if possible. This gives you an unbiased picture of the true situation.

How can I avoid misleading myself in the assessment?
You can rely on several sources to provide you with feedback about yourself:

(a) you
(b) your audience
(c) your colleagues.

REVIEWING AND IMPROVING YOUR PERFORMANCE

Once you know how well or badly you have performed, it is time to go into more detail to find out the reasons behind the results. When the reasons have been identified, action can be taken to repeat or avoid them in the future, as appropriate.

Reviewing

This is when you sit down after a presentation and ask yourself the following questions:

1. What went well?
2. Why did it go well?
3. What went wrong?
4. Why did it go wrong?

To break these questions down further, try to answer the following in relation to a presentation you have already given.

- How did the audience react?
- Could everybody in the room hear me?
- Could they all see the visual aids?
- Did I spend enough time researching the subject?
- Is my presentation confusing or well structured?
- How did I come across?
- Was the room suitable?

Can you think of four more questions you can ask yourself to review your performance?

Improving your performance

After you have identified your strengths and weaknesses, you can take some action to enhance your delivery quality. Ask yourself two questions:

(a) How can I improve on my weak points?
(b) How can I maintain my stronger points?

The answer to these questions changes the more confident you become with your presentation style. The more of an expert you become, the more difficult it is to improve on your performance. But there will always be room for improvement or a chance to try out something new.

There are many aspects of your presentation that you can consider for improvement. What about these:

- speaking too fast, no one could keep up
- too many words on the slides, no one could see
- no reminder of the previous points throughout the presentation
- body language too aggressive
- script pitched at the wrong level
- too much information for the allocated time
- totally unexpected questions, none planted.

Identify five more aspects of a presentation that you can improve.

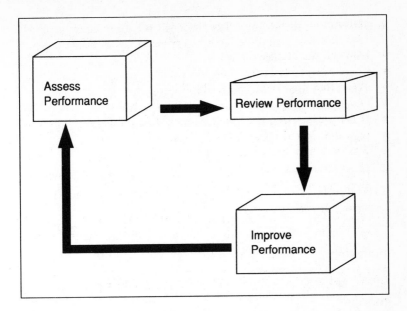

Fig. 10. The learning and improving process.

Figure 10 summarises the learning and improvement process for your presentation skills.

CREATING PRESENTATION OPPORTUNITIES

One of the most frightening activities for humans is to speak in public. It is an activity that most people try to avoid at any cost. However, when they become confident with their capabilities to present, the fear diminishes and gets converted to enjoyment.

When you start to enjoy giving presentations, you need to create new opportunities to present to keep your skills trimmed. If your job involves presenting every day, fine. If not, you need to create the opportunity to present, in order to practise your skills and enhance your career prospects.

Grabbing the opportunity

The first step towards creating a new opportunity is to grab an existing one. If you keep declining offers or requests to present, after a while the opportunities get slimmer. Here are a few suggestions on how to react when you see a presentation opportunity coming your way:

1. Determine whether it is feasible to do it with your expertise. If you are a lawyer and the opportunity is to talk about car engines, you can happily decline it.

2. Find out some more details about the event.

3. If you are interested, make it clear to the people requesting your help that you are prepared to give it.

4. If you think you can't do it on your own, get a partner to help you, and don't decline the offer straight away.

5. Always sound enthusiastic about the idea. This makes the person offering the opportunity more confident in firmly handing it over to you. In this way, you will eliminate any competition.

Creating the environment for new opportunities

If you find that time is passing and you aren't giving enough presentations, you need to do something about it. If the opportunities are not there for you to grab them, create your own. This may be done by doing one or more of the following:

- Invite your colleagues at work for a short presentation on a subject or issue of interest to them.

- If you are a member of a club or organisation, participate in events and give short presentations when appropriate without over-doing it.

- Get in touch with your old school or university and see if you can help them by giving a lecture or short talk about the work you do or the industry you are in.

- Conduct conversations with people in other departments or organisations who may be interested to know about the subject of your expertise.

- By giving good presentations in major events you may be asked by members of the audience to give a repeat somewhere else.

- In conferences and large meetings, show your enthusiasm about presenting and make sure people know what subject you know most about.

> Create a list of the events that you might use to create an opportunity to present. Then list the subjects about which you can give a presentation.

I have never been offered the opportunity to present and I can't create my own opportunities because I don't have time.
Try to create the time. Treat a presentation opportunity as part of your job. Don't treat presenting as an additional activity to your core responsibility. Remember, it helps to advance your career and you should treat it as seriously as your mainstream activity.

ENHANCING YOUR CAREER WITH EFFECTIVE PRESENTATIONS

Presenting has become one of the most important tools in business communication. It is required by most, if not all, employers as an essential skill to have in order to secure a good position in their organisation.

This means that having this skill and knowing how to use it can help you succeed in your daily operations and in your career. No matter in which field you work, you still need to present your ideas and to put them across to other people. If you work in a team, you need to transfer your knowledge and findings to your colleagues in order for them to contribute to your work when you need their assistance.

This is well known and accepted by employers and therefore, you can use your presentation skills to show them how you can contribute to their operations. So how can you do that?

- When you present, you might have several potential employers in the audience. Use the opportunity to show them how much you know about your subject and how good a communicator you are.

- If you get the opportunity to present at a high profile or important event, you can have it as a new major entry on your CV.

- Use your presentation skills in a job interview if appropriate. If you can't give a full presentation, you can always use the skills you have to come across better.

- Try to present outside your immediate job environment to expose your skills to wider audiences with potential employers.

- Remember that most successful people are good communicators, so by using your presentation skills, you make one further step towards success.

- Good presenters can be accused by jealous people of not being good at their job. Don't let this put you off. Show that you are good at both, and play down their remarks and dismiss them as a joke.

- You can only use presentations to enhance your career when you develop the confidence and the skills that deliver winning presentations. A bad presentation can have the opposite effect.

CHECKLIST

1. After every presentation, assess the results to see how well you have performed.

2. Identify your strengths and weaknesses.

3. Remember that there is always room for improvement.

4. Create new opportunities to keep your presentation skills in shape.

5. Use effective presentations to enhance your career prospects.

CASE STUDIES

Colin assesses his performance

Colin runs a small firm involved in the design of customised database and software packages. He often gives presentations to his customers on how his firm can help them solve their problems by providing them with cheap and effective solutions.

His current task is to train one of his major customers on how to use a database development tool, in order for them to be able to write the specifications for the package they want from him.

Colin cracks brilliant jokes and his audience never stop laughing.

When he assesses his performance, he decides that the feedback from the audience is great, because they laughed all the time. What he doesn't realise is that he was confusing them with his many jokes without reinforcing any of his points.

When he receives the written specifications from them, he realises that he didn't perform that well after all. Their requirements do not make sense at all.

Joy creates a new opportunity

Joy works in a bank. Her job doesn't involve presenting at all, although she was a good presenter as a student. She doesn't want to lose her good presentation skills and hopes to use them to advance her career.

One day, she visits her old university and meets a few lecturers who are happy to see her after a long time. She tells them about her job and says that as a student she always wanted to know more about the world of banking.

A senior lecturer picks up her hint and suggests that she gives a lecture to the business degree students on her experience in banking after graduation. She accepts the offer immediately and a month later gives one of her most successful presentations.

At work, everybody is pleased with her because she is establishing contact with future recruits. At university, the head of department suggests that she visits the place from time to time to maintain the link between the two establishments. The whole exercise was a very good move for Joy.

Alex improves his performance

Alex has taken on a new job as a sales representative for an office equipment supplier. His job involves giving presentations to customers and, hopefully, selling them something.

His first meeting goes wrong, although his visual aids are clear and informative, his presentation well structured and his body language and style very convincing. His problem is that he doesn't know much about the product range. A few questions make him lose the trust of his customers.

He goes back to the office to assess and review his performance. He finds out his mistake. Before the next meeting, he concentrates on finding out more about the product. He fails again. This time, he concentrated so much on improving his knowledge that he forgot about his stronger points and gave a shoddy presentation.

POINTS TO CONSIDER

1. What is the importance of performance assessment?

2. How can reviewing your performance help you?

3. What was Colin's mistake in assessing his performance?

4. What importance do presentation skills hold in securing new jobs?

5. How did Joy enhance her career prospects?

6. How could Alex have avoided his mistakes?

A FINAL WORD

I certainly hope you have enjoyed reading this book and going through the exercises. Remember that no matter how powerful presentation techniques can be, without your enthusiasm and personality put into your presentation, they will achieve little.

Finally, I wish you successful and enjoyable presentations and hope that you will always remember to be no one but yourself, when presenting.

Glossary

Acetate. Sometimes used to refer to a transparent sheet of film used to project an image from an overhead projector (see **transparency**).

Computer presentation. A presentation where visual materials are produced and presented on a computer without the need for printing. The computer screen can be connected to a projection device to enlarge the picture.

CV. Curriculum vitae. The summary of your personal, educational and work experience details.

Flannel board. A special board with a flannel surface to which pictures can be collated by pressing on.

Hue. A colour or a state of transition between two colours. Colours are identified by hues: Green, Red, Blue, etc.

Internet. A network connecting computers together worldwide. It provides access to a global library of information, where users can view or place their own messages or information on business, travel, entertainment, science and many other areas.

LCD projector. A screen projector using Liquid Crystal Display (LCD) technology, to project a digital image from a video or computer screen.

Message. What is intended to be communicated to another party.

OHP. Overhead projector. A piece of equipment consisting of a strong light, a lens and a reflecting mirror, used as a visual aid to project images on a screen.

Pause. A period of silence giving the speaker time to breathe and gather his or her thoughts.

Pixel. The smallest element on a monitor or printer.

Presentation package. A computer software package specifically designed to create and view visual aid material for presentations.

Projection. The act of projecting an image or voice. Producing a magnified version of the original state.

Rhetoric. The techniques used in public speaking to effectively persuade or influence the audience.

Script. A written copy of the contents or text.

Selling. To offer for sale, or to influence the decision of a person in a certain direction.

Skills. Natural or acquired abilities to carry out the task that requires them.

Slide. A transparent frame within which text, graphs, cartoons or diagrams can be put to be used in a presentation as visual support. The term can be used to refer to different types of positive transparent pictures, although it strictly refers to the 35 mm slides used with slide projectors.

Tablet. Another term used to refer to a view panel (see **view panel**).

Three gun projector. Projection equipment used to project digital pictures in colour, by mixing the right level of three different colour lights.

Transparency. A transparent film, used with a projector to project positive transparent images.

Unvoiced sound. A sound produced in the front of the mouth, mainly using the tongue and teeth. One such sound is produced when pronouncing the letter S.

View panel. A liquid crystal display that can be placed on an overhead projector to project a digital image from a computer monitor, when connected to it.

Voiced sound. A sound produced by the organs at the back of the mouth and the chest. For example, when pronouncing the letter A.

Further Reading

Body Language, Allan Pease (Sheldon Press).

Born to Win, James/Jongeward (Signet).

How to Manage your Boss, Hegarty/Goldberg (Ballantine).

How to Market Yourself, Ian Phillipson (How To Books).

How to Talk so People Listen, Sonya Hamlin (Thorsons).

How to Win Customers, Heinz M. Goldmann (Pan Business/Sales).

Making an After Dinner Speech, John Bowden (How To Books, 1999).

Making Effective Speeches, John Bowden (How To Books, 1998).

Managing Meetings, Ann Dobson (How To Books, 2nd Edition, 1999).

Managing Projects, James Chalmers (How To Books, 1997).

Mastering Business English, Michael Bennie (How To Books, 4th edition, 1999).

Mastering Public Speaking, Anne Nicholls (How To Books, 4th edition, 1998).

Organising a Conference, Pauline Appleby (How To Books, 1999).

Organising Effective Training, James Chalmers (How To Books, 1996).

Positive Selling, Richard Moss (Paperfronts).

Presenting Yourself for Men, Mary Spillane (Piatkus).

Presenting Yourself for Women, Mary Spillane (Piatkus).

Put it Together, Put it Across, David Bernstein (Cassell).

The Pocket Book of Quotations (Pocket Reference).

Use Your Head, Tony Bunzan (BBC).

Useful Addresses

The Chartered Institute of Marketing, Moor Hall, Cookham, Maidenhead, Berkshire SL6 9QH. Tel: (01628) 427500.

SpeakEasy Training, Premier House, 309 Ballards Lane, London N12 8NE. Tel: (0181) 446 0797.

Speak Out, 1A Rickthorne Road, Upper Holloway, London N19 4JS. Tel: (0171) 272 4473.

Index